A SWING THROUGH TIME

GOLF
IN SCOTLAND
1457-1744

Olive M. Geddes

Original edition first published in 1992
by HMSO on behalf of
The National Library of Scotland
© Crown copyright 1992

This re-designed, revised and extended
edition published in 2007 by
National Library of Scotland
George IV Bridge
Edinburgh EH1 1EW

and NMS Enterprises Limited – Publishing
National Museums Scotland
Chambers Street
Edinburgh EH1 1JF

Text: © Olive M. Geddes/National
Library of Scotland 2007

All photographs © as credited 2007

BRITISH LIBRARY CATALOGUING
IN PUBLICATION DATA
A catalogue record for this book
is available from the British Library.

PB   10 digit ISBN: 1-905267-09-6
PB   13 digit ISBN: 978-1-905267-09-5
HB   10 digit ISBN: 1-905267-18-5
HB   13 digit ISBN: 978-1-905267-18-7

Book design by Mark Blackadder.
Printed and bound in the United
    Kingdom by Cambridge Printing.

www.nls.uk   www.nms.ac.uk

---

*All images are credited individually on
the page. Every attempt has been made to
contact copyright-holders. If any images
have been inadvertently missed, please
contact the publishers.*

ARCHIE BAIRD, *page* 26
BOB GOWLAND INTERNATIONAL GOLF
    BROKERS 82
BODLEIAN LIBRARY, UNIVERSITY COLLEGE 4
THE BRITISH LIBRARY 5
THE BRITISH MUSEUM 52-53
CENTRAL LIBRARY, EDINBURGH 21, 55
EARL OF WEMYSS 35(x2), 50
GLASGOW CITY COUNCIL [MUSEUMS]
    72-73
LUFFNESS NEW GOLF CLUB 7
NATIONAL ARCHIVES OF SCOTLAND (NAS)
    vi, 2, 3, 14, 19, 83
NATIONAL GALLERIES OF SCOTLAND
    NATIONAL GALLERY OF SCOTLAND 86

SCOTTISH NATIONAL PORTRAIT GALLERY
    16, 31, 46, 78, 84
NATIONAL GALLERY, LONDON 42
NATIONAL LIBRARY OF SCOTLAND (NLS)
    8, 17, 21, 24-25, 27, 30, 33, 34(x2),
    40, 41(x3), 48, 49(x2), 51, 56, 58,
    62(x2), 66, 67, 68, 74(x2), 75, 78(x2),
    80, 86
    NLS/THE COUNTESS OF SUTHERLAND
        32(x2)
    NLS/THE HONOURABLE COMPANY OF
        EDINBURGH GOLFERS 89, 92
    NLS/*THE ILLUSTRATED LONDON NEWS*
        15
    NLS/THE ROYAL BURGESS GOLFING
        SOCIETY, EDINBURGH 17
    NLS/SIR FRANCIS OGILVY 12
NATIONAL MUSEUMS SCOTLAND i, 20, 36, 44
ROYAL AND ANCIENT GOLF CLUB,
    ST ANDREWS 64-65
SOTHEBY'S 38 (now in private ownership)

CONTENTS

ACKNOWLEDGEMENTS

TO 1992 EDITION

In writing this book, I have had much helpful advice and information from a number of colleagues and golfing authorities. Peter Lewis, Director of the British Golf Museum, St Andrews has been supportive throughout. Robert Gowland provided valuable information on early golfing equipment. Archie Baird of Gullane Golf Museum has given generously of his wealth of information on golfing history, and David Black has made many helpful suggestions. I would also like to thank my colleagues in the National Library of Scotland, particularly the staff of the Manuscript Department, for their patience and forbearance, Kenneth Gibson of the Publications Division for his help and support, also Margaret Wilkes and Ian Anderson. For photography, grateful thanks are due to Steve MacAvoy of the Library and Marius Alexander.

My thanks also go to all the private individuals and institutions who have allowed me to reproduce photographs of their documents, golfing equipment, and paintings: their names are to be found in the captions.

Olive M. Geddes, April 1992

TO THIS EDITION

A revised edition of *A Swing Through Time* has been my wish for many years. Since the book was published in 1992, the National Library of Scotland has acquired much new golfing material, notably the records of the Honourable Company of Edinburgh Golfers, probably the world's oldest Golf Club. The book has long been out of print and there have been numerous requests for copies. My grateful thanks are due to those who have made this new edition possible.

Many private individuals and institutions have again allowed me to reproduce photographs of their golfing treasures. In this new edition they are acknowledged separately overleaf.

Particular thanks are owed to Ernesto Montes and Vicky Gardner of The Treasured Library, Dallas, Texas, who suggested the additional chapter on the 'Articles and Laws of Golf' of 1744, and without whose generous support this book would not have appeared.

Lesley Taylor at NMS Enterprises Limited provided much invaluable counsel and has overseen the production of the book with infinite patience and good humour. Thanks are also due to Alexandra Miller and Julian Stone of the Library for their support and encouragement.

Olive M. Geddes, March 2007

INTRODUCTION

The origins of golf are a matter of mystery and controversy. Little, if any, evidence of the game in the form of golfing equipment or recognisable visual images survives from earlier than the mid-eighteenth century. And so, for the 'Dark Ages' of Golf – before the formalisation of the game with the establishment of the first golfing societies and clubs – it is to written sources that we must turn for reliable information.

This book takes a close look at the earliest written records of golf in Scotland, from the 1457 Act of Parliament banning the game to the first 'Rules' of golf – the 'Articles and Laws' of 1744 drawn up by the Company of Gentlemen Golfers for the competition for the Silver Club played over Leith Links.

The original documents and books, many from the collections of the National Library of Scotland, are reproduced, while transcripts, translations, commentary, and interpretation of the sources illuminate not only the early days of golf, but also the society which gave rise to the world's most internationally popular game.

This edition also includes an appendix carrying full translations where necessary, of many of the key documents featured in the book, for the benefit of those who may find them useful. Also of benefit are the guide lines which have been inserted next to many of the text images. These are intended to highlight the relevant parts of these documents.

And to support sum ...t of exp... ra... sall have ... clerk of ... be utterly ... ...

337 Item ye ...d th... ...
...

338 Anent Wapinschawingis

Item it is ordanit and decretit yt wapinschawingis be halden be ye lord baronis ... four tymes in ye ... And yt ye futball ye golf be utterly cryit doune and nocht usit ... at all prohibit ... of buttis And schuting be ... futball and ye golf ...

the mone

339 Item as to ye mone ye ... ye lordis ... the bischop ... And ye lord ... ye lord lindissay ye lord ... ye laird of ... Johne of Dalrymple or Archibald ... ye kyngis ... in ye tyme of ... mone ...

The Reformatioun of golde

340 Item ... ye Reformatioun of golde and s... to ... ye ... ...

GOLF

THE 'UNPROFFITABLE' SPORT

1457-91

Scotland in the fifteenth century was a country in turmoil, plagued by a succession of child-kings, an over-mighty and ambitious nobility, and the recurring threat of invasion from a powerful southern neighbour. Throughout the century the Scottish Kings struggled to assert their authority. In the early years James I sought to quell internal divisions and at the same time maintain an army strong enough to repel invaders by his policy of a 'firm and sure peace'. In this climate, military training was of the utmost importance, and archery practice was made compulsory for all males over twelve years of age.

It is against this background that the development of the peaceable game of golf we know today must be set, and it is from this period that the earliest known written references to the game come – references which show that, like all new games, golf met with the disapproval of the establishment.

OPPOSITE

Act of Parliament of Scotland, 6 March 1457. James II's well-known decree of 1457 banned both football and golf. This is the first known written reference to the game of golf in Scotland. (National Archives of Scotland, PA5/6)

Edinburgh, 6 March 1457: *Item it is ordaynt and decretyt ... [th]at ye fut bawe and ye golf be uterly cryt done and not usyt and [th]at ye bowe markes be maid at all parochkirkes apair of buttes and shuting be usyt ilk sunday ....*

Edinburgh, 6 March 1457: *Item, it is ordained and decreed ... that football and golf be utterly condemned and stopped and that a pair of targets be made at all parish kirks and shooting be practised each Sunday ....*

1

The earliest known written reference to golf in Scotland dates from 1457, when Parliament decreed that 'ye fut bawe and ye golf be uterly cryt done and not usyt'. Instead, the people were to practise their archery. This suggests that both golf and football were popular with the common people, if not with the authorities in fifteenth-century Scotland. Clearly the official view was that the two games were a nuisance, as well as a distraction from the practice of archery.

The 1457 Act does not specify where golf was being played, but if it was in enclosed spaces such as church yards and streets, as many golfing historians have surmised, the potential hazards can be easily imagined. As far as archery was concerned, however, there seem to have been few qualms about public safety. On the contrary, the 1457 Act reveals that target practice in the kirk yard was mandatory, and every man was to fire at least six shots at the targets set up there. Failure to do so meant a fine of two pennies, the money raised to be spent on drink to reward those who had complied with the Act.

The ban was repeated in 1471 when Parliament announced 'it is thocht expedient [th]at … ye futbal and golf be abusit in tym cumyng and ye buttes maid up and schot usit eftir ye tenor of ye act of parlyament'.[1] Similarly, in 1491, it was announced:

> … it is Statut and ordinit … that in na place of the realme be usit fut bawis gouff or uthir sic unproffitable sports, but for common gude and defence of the realme be hantit bowis schuting and markes before ordinit.[2]

James IV attempted to enforce this stern edict by imposing a collective penalty on the parish for each defiance.

Act of Parliament of Scotland, 18 May 1491. (National Archives of Scotland, PA/2/5)

    In an earlier decree of 1424, the Scottish Parliament had banned football – it is 'statut and the king forbids that na man play at the fut ball under payne of liiid [i.e. four pence]' – but had made no mention of golf. This may have been an accidental omission: James I had recently returned from 18 years of captivity in England and the Act largely reiterates an English decree of 1363 banning football. It could, however, indicate that a significant rise in the popularity of golf in Scotland had occurred sometime during the second quarter of the fifteenth century.

    It has now been established that golf, or certainly a variant of it, was being played in Europe before the game became so popular in Scotland that it was banned by Parliament. Little is known of the nature of medieval games: the Scottish Acts of Parliament may indicate that a game known as golf was being played, but they give no indication as to how it was played.

    There appears to have been a number of ball and stick games played from the Middle Ages, if not earlier. Some of these games seem to have taken place in an enclosed and defined area, and others were played in more open spaces. Some involved aiming at a target above ground, while in other cases the object was to hit the ball into a hole. These games must have constantly changed and evolved from one another over the years.

    Bede's *Life of St Cuthbert*, written towards the end of the seventh century, includes an intriguing passage on the boyhood pastimes of the young Cuthbert who grew up in the south of Scotland. 'There were one day some customary games going on in a field, and a large number of

Bede's *Life of St Cuthbert*, 12th century. In this illustration in a manuscript of Bede's *Life of St Cuthbert*, at least two ball games are taking place and a stick is clearly visible. (Bodleian Library, University College MS. 165)

boys got together, amongst whom was Cuthbert, and in the excitement of boyish whims, several of them began to bend their bodies in various unnatural forms.' No mention is made here of ball and stick games, but in an illustration relating to this specific passage in a twelfth-century manuscript of Bede's *Life* there are at least two ball games taking place and a stick is clearly visible.[3] So, to the twelfth-century mind, 'customary games' included balls and sticks.

Decrees issued by the English Parliament from 1363 to 1409 promoting archery practice and banning distracting sports, cite football as the main culprit: golf is not mentioned. There is a stained-glass window of about 1350 in Gloucester Cathedral depicting a boy playing with a club, but it can only be claimed from this that he is playing a golf-like game, and golf seems not to have reached England until the early sixteenth century.

Legend has it that 'colf', 'a golf-like game', was played at Loenen

4

aan de Vecht in the Province of North Holland in the Low Countries as early as 1297, and decrees restricting and even prohibiting 'colf' provide documentary evidence that the game was played there from the fourteenth century. In Brussels the magistrates issued an ordinance banning 'who ever plays ball with a club' in 1360, and in 1387 Albrecht of Bavaria's charter to the city of Brielle forbade gambling with four exceptions, one of which was playing 'the ball with the club without the fortifications of our afor said city'.[4]

Although there were no hard-and-fast rules at this time, it seems the game played in the Low Countries was not the same as that known in Scotland. Generally 'colf' was about aiming at above-the-ground targets, while in Scotland golf meant aiming at holes in the ground. Dutch 'colf' was often played on ice within a defined area, while the Scottish game was more wide-ranging and does not appear to have kept to a predefined course. Generally the Dutch played a 'short-game', while the Scots version was a 'long-game'.

It was not only the political authorities who disapproved of golf, but also the Church. While little documentation survives to throw light on the attitude of the pre-reformation Church in Scotland towards golf, the reformed Kirk clearly disapproved when it involved Sabbathbreaking. From about 1580 declarations to this effect were made by Kirk Sessions as far afield as Edinburgh, Perth, St Andrews, Leith, Banff, Cullen, and Stirling.

The South Leith Kirk Session records of 16 February 1610 note:

The Golf Book, c.1500. The margin of this Flemish Book of Hours shows four figures playing with clubs and what appear to be balls of wood and leather. One of the figures is kneeling to play his shot. (The British Library, Add.MS.24098)

The said day it wes concludit be the haill Sessioune, that thair sallbe na public playing suffred on the Sabbath dayes As playing at the valley bowles, at the peney stane, archerie, gowfe .... And igif any beis fund playing publicklie in ane Zaird or in the feildis upon ane Sabbath day fra morne till even That they sall pay xxs to the pure, and also make their publik repentance before the pulpite.[5]

In Humbie in East Lothian, 'James Rodger, Johne Rodger, Johne Howdan, Andrew Howdan, and George Patersone, were complained upon for playing at the golf upon ane Lord's Day' in 1651. The next day they 'were ordained to mak their public repentance [and] Johne Howdan was deposed from his office being ane deacon'.[6]

The Kirk did not always disapprove of Sunday golf as such: its concern was sometimes only with those who indulged 'in tyme of sermonis' and so were absent from church services. In the East Lothian parish of Tyninghame in the mid-seventeenth century, a group of masons called before the Kirk Session for 'playing at ze golf ... in tyme of preiching at efternoone' offered in their defence that 'thre preiching was ather done or neir endit befor they went to the lynkis'. After promising not to repeat the offence, they were merely admonished.[7]

In St Andrews the Kirk Session penalised a number of offenders who played golf 'in tyme of fast and precheing, aganis the ordinances of the kirk', and in 1599 it issued a fixed tariff of penalties. For a first offence there was a fine of ten shillings; this rose to 20 shillings for a second offence; and 'for the third fault publick repentance, and the fourt fault depravation fra their offices'.[8]

Despite the Church's attitude to golf, some clergymen were golfers themselves. In his *Historie of the Kirk in Scotland*, John Row tells of the ordeal of the Bishop of Galloway who, while playing golf on Leith Links in 1619, saw a vision of two men attacking him. Taking this as an indication of his wrong-doing in accepting the office of Bishop which he himself had previously decried, he is said to have thrown down his golf clubs, taken to his bed, and died.[9]

Golf balls are listed among the personal possessions of a number of Edinburgh merchants in the late sixteenth century.[10] These men were some of the most prominent of Edinburgh's citizens and their testaments indicate the spread and appeal of the game. Also in the 1590s, the Town Council, of which these same merchants may well have been members, objected to the defamation of the Sabbath by golfers. In 1592 the Edinburgh magistrates issued a proclamation banning games on Sundays, backing up that of the Kirk Session.[11] The fact that the Council found it necessary to add that the ban extended to its female citizens indicates that women too were enjoying the game.

J. C. Dolman, *The Sabbath Breakers*, late 19th century. These two golfers appear unpleasantly surprised to be found golfing on the links by a pair of rather stern-looking clerics. (Luffness New Golf Club)

> Seing the Sabboth day being the Lords day, it becumis everie Cristiane to dedicate himselff, his houshald, and famelie to the service and worschip of God … na inhabitants of the samyn [burgh] be themselffis thair childrein, servands or fameleis be sene at ony pastymes or gammis within or without the town upoun the Sabboth day, sic as golf, archerie, rowbowlilis [i.e. row bowls], penny stane, kaitchpullis [i.e. hand tennis] or sic other pastymes

XV. *Leith Bank*

Leith Sand

for 40 Ships of 200 Tons

Dry Dock

Draw Br

RACE

Ballast Quay

Winning Post

Distant Post

Timber

Bush

STREET

NORTH LEITH

Ship Builders Yard

Dry Dock

The Dock

C

W

Bridge

Draw Bridge

HARBOUR

THE SHORE

St BERNARDS STR.

BALTIC STR.

SALAMA

Glass Work

Glass Ho.

M

D

N

V

CONSTITUTION

Bowling Green

B

Wilkie's Row

COALL HILL

6

N

G

7

8

H

F

13

A

KIRK

KIRK YARD

15

CONSTITUTION STREET

School House

LEITH LINK

Laurie Street

Mr Giles

Mr Gile

a Common for Playing at the Golf

Casbils

MISS HOOD'S

Mr Douglas's

Mr Ried's

Bowling Green

Golf House

Mrs Hunter

Coatfield Mains
or Lock at Leith

… and als that thair dochters and wemen servands be nocht fund playing at the ball nor singing of profane sangs upoun the sam day, under sic paynes as the magestratts sall lay to thair chairge.

As with the parliamentary edicts, the Town Councils found it necessary periodically to repeat their threats of imprisonment and fines for those who failed to conform. In Edinburgh this happened the following year, in 1593, when it was declared that

… dyvers inhabitants of this burgh repaires upoun the Sabboth day to the toun of Leyth and in tyme of sermonis are sene vagand athort the streitts, drynking in tavernis, or other wayis at golf, aircherie, or other pastymes upoun the Lynks, thairby profaning the Sabboth day.[12]

Considerable fines were threatened for persistent defaulters. The earlier declaration had forbidden golf 'within or without the town', suggesting that it was expected that there might be those who would attempt to avoid the ban by leaving town; and by the 1593 edict, which specifically mentions Leith, it seems this did indeed happen.

Links are the area of open, common land along the coastal strip, which form a feature of many Scottish towns, particularly on the eastern side of the country. In the late sixteenth century, and for many years to come, they offered poor grazing and were also used for military purposes and recreation. They were in effect the people's play ground. The days of grazing cattle and drilling soldiers might have long gone, but Scotland's links golf courses are renowned throughout the world.

Leith, Edinburgh's port, lay a few miles outside the capital in the late sixteenth century. In this town, apparently because of the lax attitude of the authorities, their links were also used for recreation by the citizens of nearby Edinburgh. Leith's open, sandy links, an obvious venue for sportsmen, were used for archery and horse-racing as well as golf.

In addition to meeting with the disapproval of Parliament, the Kirk Sessions, and the Town Councils, golf also fell foul of the tradesmen's

Guilds or Incorporations. In 1690 an Elgin silversmith, Walter Hay, was fined and reprimanded for selling wine outside the church, and 'playing at ye Boulis and Golffe upoane Sundaye'.

The number of declarations forbidding golf, and their geographical spread throughout Scotland, give some indication of the game's popularity and of the reaction of those in authority to a recreation which in succeeding centuries was to become one of Scotland's great sports. That it was necessary in Scotland to ban golf by Act of Parliament in 1457, and then to repeat the ban in 1471 and 1491 on such an 'unproffitable sport', suggests that even the combined efforts of Parliament, the Town Councils, the Kirk Sessions, and the Guilds, were not entirely successful in suppressing the game.

NOTES

1 'It is thought necessary that football and golf be abandoned in future and that butts should be made up and archery practised according to the meaning of the Act of Parliament.'

2 'It is Statute and ordained ... that in no part of the country should football, golf, or other such pointless sports be practised, but for the common good and for the defence of the country archery should be practised and targets made up as previously ordained.'

3 Bodleian Library, University College (MS. 165).

4 Steven J. H. van Hengel: *Early Golf* (Liechtenstein, 1982), pp. 17-19.

5 Cited by D. Robertson: *The South Leith Records* (Edinburgh, 1911), p. 8.
'The said day it was concluded by the whole Session, that there shall be no public playing permitted on the Sabbath days such as playing at bowls, at the penny stone, archery, golf .... And if any be found playing publicly in a yard or in the fields upon a Sabbath day from morning until evening they shall pay 20 shillings to the poor, and also make their public repentance before the pulpit.'

6 John Kerr: *The Golf Book of East Lothian* (Edinburgh, 1896), p. 38.

7 Kerr, p. 37.

8 H. S. C. Everard: *A History of the Royal and Ancient Golf Club, St Andrews, from 1754-1900* (London, 1907), pp. 33-34.

9   John Row: *Historie of the Kirk in Scotland* (Maitland Club: Glasgow, 1842), pp. 81, 477.

10 Margaret Sanderson: 'Edinburgh Merchants in Society, 1570-1603', in *The Renaissance and Reformation in Scotland*, edited by Ian B. Cowan and Duncan Shaw (Edinburgh, 1983), p. 197.

11 *Extracts from the Records of the Burgh of Edinburgh, 1589-1603*, Scottish Burgh Record Society (London, 1927), p. 63.

12 *Extracts from the Records of the Burgh of Edinburgh, 1589-1603*, Scottish Burgh Record Society (London, 1927), p. 86. 'Several inhabitants of this burgh repair on the Sabbath day to the town of Leith and at times of sermons are seen wandering around the streets, drinking in taverns, or otherwise at golf, archery, or other pastimes upon the links, thereby profaning the Sabbath day.'

James the fourt
Began His Rayne
1489 He maried
Margaret eldest docht
of Henry the Sebinth

THE ROYAL
GAME

1502-1682

While the Scottish Kings had previously ratified Acts which forbade their subjects to play golf, by at least the early sixteenth century they had no inhibitions about playing the game themselves.

There may well have been political reasons for this change in attitude. James IV came to the throne in 1488 at the age of 15. By 1502 he had made a peace treaty with the English King, Henry VII, and in 1503 he married Henry's daughter, Margaret, at Holyrood Abbey in Edinburgh. Peace with England seems to have resulted in military training being considered less essential, and consequently games and pastimes became more acceptable.

Evidence that the Scottish Kings played golf is provided by the Accounts kept by David Beaton of Creich, Lord High Treasurer of Scotland. Expenses for the minutiae of domestic life in the royal household appear, and James's varied interests are well represented: included are payments for books, equipment for the King's chemical experiments, entertainments for the court, as well as for outdoor pursuits such as golf, hunting, archery, horse-racing, bowls and tennis.

OPPOSITE
James IV and Queen Margaret from the *Seton Armorial*, 1591. James IV, the golfing King, is depicted with his English Queen, Margaret, daughter of Henry VII. The sumptuously illustrated *Seton Armorial* was made in 1591 for Robert, 6th Lord Seton, who later became 1st Earl of Winton. (National Library of Scotland and Sir Francis Ogilvy, Acc.9309)

James IV spent the month of February 1503 entirely in Edinburgh, and as the illustration from the Lord High Treasurer's Accounts shows, he purchased golf clubs and balls on the 6th of that month. The three French crowns the King spent on 3 February, 'to play at the golf with the Earl of Bothwell', almost certainly suggest they had a wager on the match and that the King lost. There is no indication as to where in Edinburgh they played or how they played.

The King's games of golf in Edinburgh were clearly not isolated incidents, as the Treasurer's Accounts also note expenditure on golf in Perth in 1502, and in 1506, at which time James was probably in St Andrews. The 1506 entry is of added interest for the relative cost of golf balls and clubs at the time. The clubs bought for the King cost one shilling each, while the balls were three for a shilling.

Credit for introducing golf to England may well be due to James IV and his court following his marriage to Princess Margaret in 1503, as the game seems to have been known in England by 1513. In that year, Henry VIII's Queen, Katharine of Aragon, wrote in a letter to Cardinal Wolsey that 'all … [the King's] subjects be very glad, I thank God, to be busy at the golf'.[1]

James IV's successors on the Scottish throne were also golfers. His son, James V, is believed to have played at Gosford in East Lothian, and

King James V is said to have been fond of Gosford, and … it was suspected by his contemporaries, that, in his frequent excursions to that part of the country, he had other purposes in view besides golfing and archery. Three favourite ladies, Sandilands, Weir and Oliphant, one of whom resided at Gosford and the others in the neighbourhood, were often visited by their Royal and gallant admirer.[2]

legend has it that Mary, Queen of Scots played at St Andrews, as depicted in the Edwardian illustration below. Unfortunately, there is no firm documentary evidence to show that Mary was among the first lady golfers, and the Lord High Treasurer's Accounts for her reign omit any reference to purchases of golf balls and clubs.

What has survived, however, are claims by Mary's enemies that she failed to behave as a royal widow should after the murder of her second husband, Lord Darnley, at Kirk o' Fields in February 1567. One of the misdemeanours referred to was her alleged indulgence in a game of golf in the grounds of Seton Palace in East Lothian within a few days of Darnley's death.

In his *Rerum Scoticarum Historia*, George Buchanan rails against Mary, claiming that she indulged in 'sports that were clearly unsuitable to women'.[3] Mary's half-brother, James Stewart, the Earl of Moray, who admittedly did not care for the Queen very much, was more specific in the 'Articles' he put before the Westminster Commissioners on 6 December 1568:

Mary, Queen of Scots, on the Links at St Andrews (Illustrated London News, 1905). Tradition has it that Mary, Queen of Scots played golf on the links at St Andrews. (National Library of Scotland, NJ.677)

Few dayes eftir the murther remaning at halyrudehous, she past
to seytoun, exercing hir one day richt oppinlie at the feildis with
the palmall and goif, And on the nicht planelie abusing hir body
with boithuell.[4]

According to Lord Moray, Mary played golf and 'palmall' at Seton
shortly after Darnley's death, and dallied there with the Earl of Bothwell,
the prime suspect in the explosion at Kirk o' Fields. 'Palmall' would seem
to be the French game of *jeu-de-mail* or *paille-maille*. In one form it
resembled croquet, but there was also a long-driving cross-country form
of the game, similar to golf.

Leaving aside Mary's morals and the question of Darnley's sudden
death, these extracts reveal something of attitudes towards women's golf

ABOVE
Alexander Keirinix, *Seton
Palace and the Forth
Estuary*, *c*.1635-40. Seton
Palace, East Lothian, where
Mary, Queen of Scots, is
said to have played golf
with the Earl of Bothwell
shortly after the death of
her husband, Lord
Darnley, in suspicious
circumstances in 1567.
The remains of the Palace
were demolished in 1789
to make way for the present
Adam house. (Scottish
National Portrait Gallery)

INSTITUTED A.D. 1608.

in the sixteenth century, when it would seem to have been considered as frivolous, slightly risqué, and certainly not a ladylike sport.

Mary's son, James VI and I, also took an interest in golf. Traditionally he is believed to have learnt on the North Inch of Perth, and may well have continued to play in England when the Scottish court moved to London on James's accession to Elizabeth I's throne in 1603. He has been associated with the foundation of the Royal Blackheath Golf Club in 1608. The Club's records, however, were destroyed by fire in the late eighteenth century, and there is no documentary evidence for its existence prior to 1787.[5]

Although golf is not mentioned in the *Basilikon Doron*, James's instructions to his son, Prince Henry, in which he recommends games to 'exercise the engine', the young prince was probably a golfer. It is recorded that on one occasion he came close to accidentally striking his schoolmaster with a raised club.[6] It has been claimed that a painting by an unknown Flemish artist, depicting a child with a golf club and ball, is Prince Henry, thus lending weight to the argument for the Dutch origin of the game.[7] However, both the age of the child, and the Breda medal he is wearing, make this improbable. Undoubtedly there were close ties between the royal houses of Scotland and the Netherlands, and a representative of the States General stood godfather at the young Prince's christening at Stirling in 1549. Nonetheless, Dutch merchants traded in many countries. That golf did not flourish in East Anglia, for example, where they were frequent visitors, indicates that cultural and trading contacts with the Low Countries were not necessarily the reason for the development of golf in Scotland.

There is evidence that James VI and I took an interest in the developing trade in golfing equipment. William Mayne, 'bower burgess' of Edinburgh, was appointed royal club-maker for life, and in 1618 James gave the patent of golf ball-making in Scotland to James Melville for 21 years in favour of the ball-maker William Berwick, to 'furnische the said kingdom with better golf balls'.

In the Letters of Licence of 1618, James shows his awareness of the importance of the game to the Scottish economy when he states that 'no small quantity of gold and silver is transported yearly out of his heines [His Highness's] kingdome of Scotland for bying of golf ballis'. No indication of the source of these balls is given, but it seems likely to have been the Low Countries, as Dutch toll-registers for Bergen op Zoom for 1486 record that 'Ritsaert' [Richard] Clays paid six groats for exporting a barrel of golf balls to Scotland. Further examples of balls bought for sale in Scotland are recorded for 1494, 1495 and 1496.[8]

Ball-making was organised as a trade in the Low Countries from the mid-sixteenth century when there is known to have been a system of apprenticeship in existence. In Goirle, a town whose inhabitants are still known by their nickname of 'ball-stuffers', a ball-maker is mentioned in a document of 1552. So prolific were the town's ball-makers that they

Letters of Licence to James Melville, 1618. In 1618 James VI and I gave the patent of golf ball-making in Scotland to James Melville, Quarter-master to the Earl of Morton. (National Archives of Scotland, PS1/87, ff.169-70)

were able to give immediate assistance to the nearby village of Tilburg when Sebastian van Warendrop, the army commander of the Duke of Parma in the Spanish War, demanded a ransom of 12,000 golf balls in 1588.[9]

It is not stated what type of balls were being made in Goirle at this time. If the Dutch game was played primarily on ice, it would require a very different ball from the featherie, as it would need to float, or at least not become misshapen through constant contact with ice. Wooden golf balls, such as the boxwood balls dating from the mid-sixteenth century found under a house in Amsterdam, would have been suitable.

James Melville, given the patent of golf ball-making in Scotland by James VI and I in 1618, is unlikely to have been a ball-maker himself, as he was Quarter-master to the Earl of Morton. He had partners and assistants who could lease his rights to craftsmen, but, in accordance with the terms of the monopoly, every ball produced had to bear Melville's stamp, and he was authorised to seek out and confiscate illegal ones. An entry in the Register of the Privy Council of Scotland for 1629, however, reveals that the patent was never enforced.

In that year William Dickson and Thomas Dickson, golf ball-makers in Leith, complained to the Privy Council against James Melville for

… pretending he has a gift from his Majesty's late father, for exacting a 'certain impost aff everie gowffe ball made within this kingdome' which gift their Lordships had never ratified, and on 20th February last, he sent a number of 'lawlesse souldiers … who after manie threatnings and execrable oathes … tooke frome thame ane greate number of gowffe ballis quhilkis [which] they had made for his Majesteis use at the desire of Arthure Naismith, indweller in Edinburgh'.

The outcome was that 'the Lords find that James Melville and his servants took nineteen gowffe ballis from the pursuers most unwarrantably'. Melville was fined and cautioned.[10]

The reign of Charles I, the last Stuart monarch born in Scotland, was a turbulent one which saw the religious upheavals of the Covenanting Movement in Scotland, the English Civil War, the King's flight to the Continent, his return and his subsequent capture. It ended dramatically with the King's execution in 1649. Nonetheless, in the midst of all this upheaval there were more peaceful moments, and when Charles received the news of the 1641 Irish Rebellion, legend has it that he was playing golf on Leith Links.

It was on the same links at Leith that what has been dubbed the first golf 'international' is said to have been played in 1681. The then Duke of York, later James VII, spent some time in Scotland between 1680 and 1682 as the King's Commissioner, residing at Holyroodhouse with his Duchess and, for part of the time, his daughter, the future Queen Anne. Tradition relates that he challenged two English noblemen to a game of golf following their claim that it was an English sport.

The Duke chose as his partner John Paterson, a cordiner or cobbler, and local golf champion. The Scots won the day, and the prize money enabled Paterson to acquire the house in the Canongate of Edinburgh which later became known as Golfer's Land. Legend has it that the Duke caused an escutcheon to be fixed on the house depicting a crest with the ducal hand holding a golf club and bearing the motto 'Far and Sure'. Golfer's Land no longer stands, but a commemorative plaque has been placed on a nearby property.

As a postscript to this story, the Edinburgh Town Council minutes for 1723 show that George Fenwick, a brewer in Leith, had the right to a newly-built house on the South Leith Links feued by the town to the

James Drummond's *Golfer's Land, Canongate, Edinburgh*, *c*.1850. The house in the Canongate of Edinburgh which John Paterson supposedly had built following victory in the first golfing 'international' between Scotland and England. (Central Library, Edinburgh)

deceased John Paterson, Cordiner on the Canongate, for five merks or a set of golf clubs yearly to the Provost. The Council chose the clubs.[11]

Golf may have been banned by Act of Parliament, by Burgh Councils and by Kirk Sessions, but given that many of the Stuart Kings themselves played this so-called 'unproffitable sport', to attempt to ban the game can only have been a forlorn hope. Indeed, golf would seem to have been a deeply rooted national pastime for king and commoner alike from the sixteenth century onwards.

NOTES

1 Robert Browning: *A History of Golf* (London, 1955), p. 2.

2 Neil Roy: 'Topographical Description of the Parish of Aberlady', in *Transactions of the Society of Antiquaries of Scotland*, 1872, pp. 517-18.

3 Cited in W. A. Gatherer: *The Tyrannous Reign of Mary, Queen of Scots* (Edinburgh, 1958), p. 120.

4 'Staying at Holyroodhouse for a few days after the murder, she then went to Seton, taking exercise one day right openly in the fields with palmall and golf, and at night clearly dallying with Bothwell.' (British Library, Add.MS.33531)

5 Ian T. Henderson and David I. Stirk: *Royal Blackheath* (London, 1981).

6 British Library, Harleian MS.6391.

7 Ian T. Henderson and David I. Stirk: *Golf in the Making* (London, 1979), p. 8.

8 van Hengel, p. 51.

9 van Hengel, pp. 29-30.

10 *Register of the Privy Council of Scotland*, 1629-30, vol. III, second series (Edinburgh, 1901), p. 174.

11 C. E. S. Chambers: 'Early Golf at Bruntsfield and Leith', in *Book of the Old Edinburgh Club*, vol. XVIII (Edinburgh, 1932), p. 10.

JAMES
MELVILLE

THE ST ANDREWS STUDENT

1574

An early golfing historian, Sir Walter Simpson, writing in the mid-nineteenth century, surmised that golf in St Andrews started when a shepherd idly hit a stone into a hole with his crook.[1] There is no firm evidence to substantiate this speculation, and written records of St Andrews golf date from 1552. Then, in an Acknowledgement of permissions granted to him by the Town Council, John Hamilton, Bishop of St Andrews, reserved to the people of the Burgh the right to use the links for 'golfe, futeball, shuting and all games', indicating golf was already popular in the town.[2] According to Dutch documentary sources, there was trade in golfing equipment between Scotland and the Low Countries in the late sixteenth century: merchants from the Netherlands, Norway and France are known to have visited the annual Senzie Fair in St Andrews, held between 1350 and 1581, where it is tempting to suppose golf may have been one of their leisure activities.[3]

One of the most interesting documents to have survived from the early days of golf in St Andrews is a diary kept by a student at the University there.[4] James Melville was the son of the Minister of Maryton, near Montrose, on the north-east coast of Scotland. The nephew of the better known Andrew Melville, the famous preacher and theologian, he was a student between 1569 and 1574. Later he became Minister of Kilrenny in Fife, and was elected Moderator of the General Assembly of the Church of Scotland in 1589. He died in Berwick-upon-Tweed in 1614 while imprisoned by Charles I for his staunch opposition to that monarch's reintroduction of bishops into Scotland.

Plan of St Andrews, attributed to John Geddy, *c.*1580. Although this plan of St Andrews emphasises the important educational and ecclesiastical buildings at the eastern end of the town, the links to the west, where James Melville probably played his golf, are clearly shown. (National Library of Scotland, MS.20996)

For much of his eventful life, James Melville kept a diary. In this closely-written volume, which could more accurately be described as his 'memoirs', Melville gives important information about ecclesiastical and political happenings in Scotland from the presbyterian point of view at a turbulent time in the country's history, and it is for this that the diary is largely known. However, he also noted details of his personal and family life, providing us with a rare insight into daily life outside the classroom for a student at St Andrews in the late sixteenth century.

By his own account, James Melville appears to have been a hard-working and eager student, although, endearingly, he does record that when he first arrived classes might end in tears. He tells us he was neither well-grounded in Latin grammar, nor particularly mature, and so failed to understand the Latin lessons: 'I did nathing bot bursted and grat ... and was of mynd to haiff gone ham agean.' Melville appears soon to have overcome his early problems and seems to have enjoyed his years as a student. He even found time for games, one such being golf.

In his diary, in addition to noting details of the academic courses he attended, his tutors, and visits to St Andrews from notables such as John Knox, Melville recorded his recreations. At school in Montrose the young Melville had been 'teached to handle the bow for archerie, the glub [club] for goff, the batons for fencing, also to rin [run], to loope [jump], to swoom [swim], to warsle [wrestle]'. While he does not seem to have had a great deal of pocket money, Melville tells us that his father provided him with the means to purchase his 'necessars'. Thus the young James had bow and arrows for archery, and club and balls for golf. Fatherly approval, however, did not extend to 'Catchpull and Tauern', that is, hand tennis and drinking in taverns, but 'now and then' he was able to play a game of 'racket catche', another form of tennis.

No details are given in the diary of golfing equipment available in the St Andrews of 1574, save that James Melville had 'club and balls', indicating that the game was perhaps played using a single club. Generally, little is known of the construction of early golf clubs: they may well have been made from one piece of wood cut out of a hedgerow. It is clear from later accounts, however, that the heads and shafts of clubs were made from different woods, as heads were indeed replaced.

A golf club needed to have two main properties: a head of hardwood capable of withstanding many strikes of the ball, and also a whippy or springy shaft. These properties did not occur together in any natural British timber. A one-piece club would need to have a springy shaft. Springy timber, by its very nature, is easy to split or cleave, thus a one-piece ash club would have a springy shaft but a head that would easily split after a few strokes. The earliest clubs that survive have hawthorn heads and, most commonly, ash or alder shafts, although Thomas Kincaid, writing in Edinburgh in 1687, recommended hazel.[5] Lancewood or lemonwood has also been recorded, certainly from the seventeenth century.[6]

Golf club heads from the Low Country, 17th century. (Archie Baird)

For practical reasons, more than one ball was required, and it seems likely they were made from a hardwood such as turned boxwood. In an account of the siege of Kirkwall Castle in Orkney in 1614, the Earl of Caithness tells of 'cannone billets [bullets] … brokkin lyke goulfe balls upoune the castelle'. Cannon balls would split into separate pieces like wooden balls, whereas leather balls would only split at the seams. The evidence from the Continent at this time, from both pictures and documents, is that there, too, wooden balls were used.[7]

James Melville does not tell us where he played his golf. However, Bishop Hamilton's Acknowledgement of 1552 indicates that the links were a popular golfing ground in St Andrews as elsewhere, and it would seem likely that Melville played his golf there. Yet, in spite of the evidence for the emergence of designated areas for the game from the sixteenth century, there are records which indicate that, inevitably, golf continued to be played within towns and villages for some time to come.

As late as 1632 the Books of Adjournal, the record of the Justiciary Court, tell of the death of a Kelso man, Thomas Chatto, 'within the kirk zaird of Kelso upon the first day of Februar last be geving him ane deidlie straik with ane golf ball struckin out with ane golf club under his left lug'. This incident happened during a 'bonspill at the golf within the said kirk zaird', when the unfortunate Chatto was 'lurking' in the church yard at the time of the match. It seems likely that he was merely an innocent bystander.[8]

The evidence as to where golfers played in Scotland prior to the eighteenth century is contradictory, and it seems they sometimes went to open spaces and at other times played in confined areas. Possibly, the game was played in the streets by small children, or by people who did not have the time to go out to a field or to the links for a proper game. It is hardly surprising that, removed from the thoroughfares, golf was regarded more favourably as a pleasant recreation.

ABOVE
Diary of James Melville, 1574. This entry in James Melville's diary for 1574 is one of the earliest references to golf in St Andrews. (National Library of Scotland, Adv.MS.34.4.15, p. 25.)

Als I haid my necessars honestlie aneuche of my father bot nocht els; for archerie and goff I haid bow arrose glub and bals, but nocht a purss for Catchpull and Tauern, sic was his fatherlie wesdom for my weill. Yit now and then I lernit and usit sa mikle bathe of the hand and racket catcheas might serue for moderat and halsome exerceise of the body.

Also, I had my necessaries honestly enough from my father but nothing else; for archery and golf I had bow arrows club and balls, but not money for hand tennis or drinking, such was his fatherly wisdom for my well-being. Yet now and then I learned and used so much of racket tennis as might serve for moderate and wholesome exercise of the body.

NOTES

1   Sir Walter Simpson: *The Art of Golf* (Edinburgh, 1887).

2   H. S. C. Everard: *A History of the Royal and Ancient Golf Club of St Andrews* (Edinburgh, 1907), pp. 28-30.

3   van Hengel, p. 12.

4   National Library of Scotland, Adv.MS.34.4.15. For a more detailed discussion of James Melville's diary, see *The Diary of Mr James Melville*, Bannatyne Club (Edinburgh, 1829).

5   Diary of Thomas Kincaid, National Library of Scotland, Adv.MS.32.7.7. See below, pp. 52-61.

6   I am indebted to Robert Gowland for information concerning early golf clubs.

7   Douglas Young: *St Andrews: Town and Gown, Royal and Ancient* (London, 1969), p. 122.

8   *Selected Judiciary Cases, 1624-50*, Stair Society (Edinburgh, 1953), vol. 1, p. 204.

A SCHOOLBOYS'
GRAMMAR

Much of the early evidence for golf in Scotland has so far concentrated on the development of the game in the south and east of the country. There is evidence, however, from records of Town Councils and of Kirk Sessions, and the papers of Incorporations and of private individuals, to indicate that golf was also played in the north from at least the sixteenth century.

The Aberdeen Burgh Records mention golfers in the streets as early as 1538, and in 1613 note the conviction of John Allan, bookbinder, 'for setting ane goiff ball in the kirk yeard, and striking the same against the kirk'. Possibly this was merely an act of malice, but perhaps the church door was being used as a target. In 1625 soldiers are recorded as exercising 'in the principall pairt of the linkes betwixct the first hole and the Queen's hole'.[1] This would indicate that the game had developed considerably by this time, with a multiplicity of fixed named holes.

Further north, Sir Robert Gordon of Gordonstoun enthused over the links at Dornoch in his 'Genealogy of the Earls of Sutherland' of 1628, describing them as 'the fairest and lairgest links (or grein feilds) of any part in Scotland'. In Sir Robert's opinion, 'They do far surpasse the feilds off Montrois or Saint andrews'. Perhaps this assertion of Dornoch's superiority should not be taken at face value, as he goes on to state:

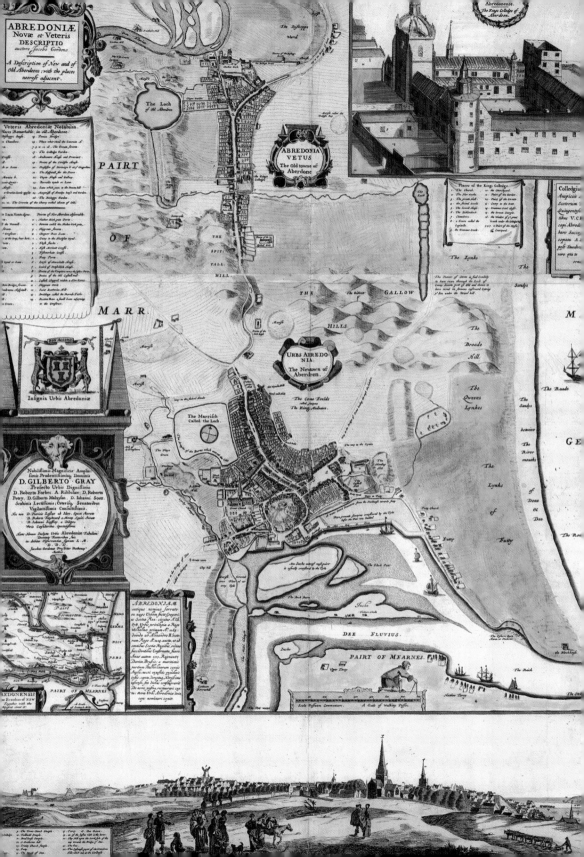

Along the sea-coast are 'the fairest and lairgest links (or grein feilds) of any part in Scotland, fit for archerie, goffing, ryding, and all other exercise; They do far surpasse the feilds off Montrois or Saint andrews.

Robert Gordone

Ther is not a rat in Sutherland, and if they do come thither in shippes from other parts (which often happeneth) they dye presenttlie how soone they do smell of the aire of that countrey, and (which is strange) there is great store anfd aboundance of them in Catheynes, the very next adiacent province.[2]

It is not known if Sir Robert was himself a golfer, but he was probably a competent archer as he won the prize of a Silver Arrow in a competition at the Palace of Holyroodhouse in 1617 (see p. 87). This was organised during James VI and I's first visit to Scotland following his accession to the English throne. On the death of John, Earl of Sutherland, in 1615, Sir Robert became Tutor or Guardian to his young nephew, John, now himself Earl of Sutherland. Sir Robert's accounts as Tutor, now in the National Library of Scotland, include payments for golfing equipment

OPPOSITE
James Gordon of Rothie-may, *Aberdeen New and Old, c.*1647. (National Library of Scotland, EMS.s.249)

ABOVE
Unknown artist, *Sir Robert Gordon, 1580-1656.* Courtier at the courts of James VI and I and Charles I [detail]. (Scottish National Portrait Gallery)

31

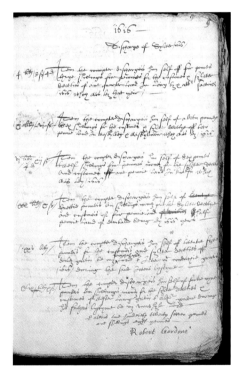

Item ten poundis guven this yeir for bowes, arrowes, golff clubbes, and balls, with other necessars for his L[ordship's] exercise.

for the young Earl while at school in Dornoch. In 1619, £10 was spent 'this yeir for bowes, arrowes, golff clubbes, and balls with other necessars for his L[ordship's] exercise'.[3]

Golf is also known to have been played in Orkney in the seventeenth century. In 1685 James Dickson, writing from Kirkwall, requested a friend to 'remember to bring with [him] one dozen of common golf ballis to me and David Moncrieff'. Similarly, there are references to golf in the journal of a seventeenth-century Orkney skipper, Patrick Traill of Elness.[4]

It is from Aberdeen, however, in what at first seems to be a rather unlikely source, that one of the most interesting and detailed documents relating to the development of golf in seventeenth-century Scotland appears, namely David Wedderburn's schoolboys' 'Grammar'.

In about 1636, David Wedderburn, Master of Aberdeen Grammar School, prepared a Latin Grammar for his pupils[5] (see page 34). As conversation at the school was conducted in Latin, there was a need for the pupils to be taught the Latin for words they might use every day. In the *Vocabula*, Wedderburn seems to have attempted to motivate his pupils by including Latin words and phrases for a variety of sports, one such being golf. Football, archery and bowls are given similar treatment, indicating the range of sporting activities available to Aberdeen schoolboys in the mid-seventeenth century. The short section on golf, headed 'Baculus', meaning 'club', provides a detailed, and often humorous,

The Prospect of Old Aberdeen, from John Slezer's *Theatrum Scotiae* (London, 1693). (National Library of Scotland, EMS.b.5.1)

description of the game. Its importance lies in the fact that here, for the first time, we are given some indication of how golf was played at the time:

BACULUS

Baculus, pila clavaria, a Golf Ball; *Fovea*, a Goat [bunker]; *Percute pilam baculo: Nimis curtasti hunc missum*, This is too short a stroak; *Pila tua devia est: Procul excussisti pilam*, This is a good stroak, *Statumina pilam arena*, Teaz [tee up] your Ball on the sand; *Statumen*, The Teaze; *Frustra es*, That is a miss, *vel irritus hic conatus est. Percute pilam, sensim*, Give the Ball but a little chap. *Apposite*, That is very well. *Immissa est pila in Foveam*, the Ball is goated. *Quomodo eum hinc elidam. Cedo baculum ferreum.* Let see the Bunkard Club. *Iam iterum frustra es*, that is the second miss. *Tertio, quarto, etc. Bene tibi cessit hic ictus*, That is well stricken. *Male tibi cessit hic ictus. Huc recta pilam dirige: Dirige recta versus foramen*, Strike directly upon the hole. *Percute pilam sursum versus*, Strike up the hill: *Percute deorsum versus*, Strike down the hill: *Ah praeterlapsa est foramen; Factum quod volui*, I would not wish a better stroak; *Immissa est in paludem*, It is in the Myre: *Recta evolavir*, It hath flown directly on. *Baculi caput*, the head of the Club. *Baculi caulis*, The Club shaft. *Baculi manubrium*, The handle where the wippen [grip] is, *Baculi filum*, The wippen.

John Allan's conviction for striking a golf ball against the kirk door in Aberdeen in 1613, shows that the game was still played in the town in the early seventeenth century. As in Edinburgh and St Andrews, the evidence as to where golf was played is contradictory, and the *Vocabula*, with its description of the playing surface, and references to up the hill and down the hill, as well as the words for holes and bunkers, and sand for teeing off, indicates that, in 1636, Aberdeen schoolboys were playing

David Wedderburn, *Vocabula* (Aberdeen, 1713). Frontispiece and extract from the 1713 edition of Wedderburn's Latin Grammar, first published in 1636. The passage headed 'Baculus' ('club'), provides a detailed, often humorous description of the game of golf. (National Library of Scotland, LC.445[2])

their golf on the coastal links. This is confirmed by James Gordon of Rothiemay's *'Aberdoniae Utriusque Descriptio Topographica'* of 1661. He writes of the links: 'Here the inhabitants recreate themselves with several kinds of exercises, such as football, golf, bowling and archery. Here likewise they walk for their health.'[6]

Golf on the links would at first have been a cross-country sport, with players starting at one man-made or natural feature and attempting to reach another in the fewest number of strokes. Only when the game developed to the point where individual holes were generally recognised by players, did golf courses as such emerge. Much of the information in the *Vocabula* regarding the playing surface appears in print probably for the first time, and indicates how the development of the game was influenced by the use of Scotland's eastern coastal strips or links. Bunkers and sand for teeing off, or teazing, are appropriate to links courses. The former occur naturally through the action of wind on the sandy surface, but their potential as a hazard in the game was quickly realised and they were later incorporated in man-made courses.

There has been some controversy regarding the use of tees, as the earliest 'Rules of Golf' laid down by the Company of Gentlemen Golfers in 1744 (see page 91) state that 'your tee must be on the ground'. Thomas Kincaid, writing in Edinburgh in 1687-88, however, appears to have used the method known to Wedderburn; he recommended that, when learning to drive, the player should 'tie [tee] [their] ball at first pretty high from the ground'.[7]

Items of golfing equipment are also referred to by Wedderburn, revealing that golf in Aberdeen was no longer a one club game, as different clubs for different shots are mentioned. The Dutch poet, Bredero, also tells of a choice of clubs available to the early seventeenth-century 'kolver' or golfer. These were either a club of ash weighted with lead, or 'syne schotse kilk' (i.e. his Scottish club), probably made of boxwood with lead in the heel to give weight.

In Wedderburn's Aberdeen, a *'baculus fereus'* or iron-headed club was in use. This is described here as the 'bunkard club', presumably the club used to get out of a bunker. Iron-headed clubs of the time were crude

UPPER CLUB
A square toe iron with a curved face, probably late 17th century. (Earl of Wemyss)

LOWER CLUB
A heavy or deep faced spur toe iron, mid-17th century. (Earl of Wemyss)

and heavy, and were liable to burst expensive featherie balls. It seems likely they were used as a last resort to hit out of bunkers or very rough ground. Also of interest are the words given for different parts of the club: *'baculi caput'* is the head of the club, and *'baculi caulis'* the shaft, indicating the arrival of jointed clubs. It would seem the head and shaft were bound together with some form of fabric, the 'wippen'. Wedderburn also says the 'wippen' was on the handle, and the word seems to refer either to the fabric over the joint between head and shaft, or to the grip.

A golf ball is described here as a *'pila clavaria'*, that is a ball like a skull. This is a featherie ball, the stitching of which resembled the bones on the top of the head. The featherie consisted of segments of leather, usually three, sewn together to form a bag and then stuffed with feathers, traditionally sufficient to fill the crown of a top hat. The pressure created added considerably to the ball's liveliness, and a well made featherie represented a significant technological advance on the earlier wooden balls. The featherie was not without its faults: it quickly became sodden and heavy in wet conditions, easily lost its shape, and was liable to burst when miss-hit on a seam with an iron club. Featheries were also very expensive, as a ball-maker could only make three or four in a day. Despite this, the featherie is of great importance, and was favoured until the mid-nineteenth century when it was replaced by the gutta ball.

The evidence as to the construction of golf balls in the late sixteenth and early seventeenth centuries is contradictory. The papers of the Canongate Cordiners (or Cobblers) of Edinburgh refer to a dispute with the 'gouffball makers' of Leith in 1554 when the inference was that the cordiners were illegally stitching leather balls, but no further details of the construction of these balls is given. Featherie balls as such are known to have been in use by 1618 when James VI and I granted the 21-year monopoly of the golf ball trade in Scotland to James Melville (see chapter 'The Royal Game', pp. 18-20), and it would seem safe to say a variety of balls were in use including wooden and stitched leather balls.

Featherie golf balls. (National Museums Scotland)

36

In 1642, by which time Melville's monopoly had expired, Aberdeen had its own golf ball-maker, John Dickson of Leith. He was a member of the rival firm of golf ball-makers who had complained to the Privy Council about Melville's high-handed actions in 1629. This unpleasantness behind him, Aberdeen Burgh Council gave Dickson a 'licence … of making gouff balls during the concils pleasure and his gude carage and behaviour, bacause there is no such tradesmen in this burgh and [he] has a testificat from Leith of his bygane life and conversation among them'.[8] By the mid-seventeenth century, golf balls were being made in several Scottish burghs including Leith, St Andrews and Montrose, as well as Aberdeen.

The *Vocabula* reveals that a variety of strokes were in use in 1636, including short strokes or putts and strokes up the hill and down the hill. Wedderburn also gives a number of common phrases for use when on the course. Most, such as *'Bene tibi cessit hic ictus'* – 'Well struck!' – might still be heard today, although it is to be hoped that modern players do not need to use the phrase *'Immissa est in paludem'* – 'It's in the myre!'.

NOTES

1 *Extracts from the Accounts of the Burgh of Aberdeen*, Old Spalding Club (Aberdeen, 1852, *et seq.*).

2 National Library of Scotland, Dep.314/2.

3 National Library of Scotland, Dep.313/1597.

4 B. H. Hossack, *Kirkwall in the Orkneys* (Kirkwall, 1900), pp. 125, 129.

5 David Wedderburn's *Vocabula* (Aberdeen, 1636). For a more detailed discussion, see David Hamilton: *Early Aberdeen Golf* (Glasgow and Oxford, 1985).

6 James Gordon's manuscript is in the National Library of Scotland, Adv.MS.34.2.8, f.98. For a transcription, see Cosmo Innes: *A Description of both Towns of Aberdeen*, in the Old Spalding Club (Edinburgh, 1842).

7 For Thomas Kincaid's diary, see below, pp. 52-61.

8 Aberdeen Burgh Records.

'POOR MASTER GALL'

PERTH

1638

In 1638 Henry Adamson's *The Muses Threnodie, or Mirthfull Mournings on the Death of Master Gall* was published in Edinburgh.[1] Adamson's verses are among the earliest printed works to mention golf. They also confirm that the game was popular in Perth in the lifetime of James Gall, the 'Master Gall' of the title.

This is not the earliest known reference to golf in Perth, as according to the Lord High Treasurer for Scotland's Accounts, James IV paid 14 shillings in 1502 for clubs from a 'bowar' or bow-maker in St Johnston, or Perth.[2] As bow-makers were used to working in wood, it has been assumed that they had the skill and the equipment necessary to make wooden golf clubs, and that as demand for bows and arrows declined, so club-making took over. There is no written evidence to substantiate this, but it is known that later, when iron clubs became more common, they were made by blacksmiths.

The Lord High Treasurer's Accounts do not indicate where in Perth James IV played his golf. Situated on the banks of the Firth of Tay, Perth is not a coastal town and has no links. The town's Kirk Session minutes from 1592, however, make reference to golf on the Muirton meadows,

OPPOSITE

Jan Anthonisz van Ravesteyn, *Portrait of a young boy with a golf club and ball*, 1626.

(Original permission from Sotheby's; painting now in private ownership)

Item, the xxi day of September, to the bowar of Sanct Johnstoun for clubbes xiiijs [14 shillings].

near to the North Inch, and King James IV may well have played there.

In his poem of 1638, Henry Adamson mourns the death of his friend, James Gall, whom he describes fulsomely as 'a citizen of Perth, and a gentleman of goodly stature, and pregnant wit, much given to pastimes such as golf, archerie, and curling; and Joviall companie'. Master Gall was a committed sportsman who regularly played golf, shot and curled. If the proportion of the poem devoted to the respective sports is any indication, archery was his first love, but golf and curling seem to have come a close second.

A footnote to the 1774 edition of Henry Adamson's lament for his friend elaborates on the subject of golf:

> Perth stands in the middle of a beautiful green about an English mile in length, where the citizens for ages have exercised themselves during the spring and autumnal seasons with golf clubs and balls. The pastime is interrupted during the summer months by the luxuriency of the grass ... milch cows, etc.

In the Low Countries too, golf was played largely from autumn until spring, partly because in the summer the long grass made it difficult to locate balls. In 1483, however, the Mayors of Haarlem granted the mowing rights of the golf course to the 'Masters of the Hours' of the

And yee my Clubs, you must no more prepare
To make you bals flee whistling in the aire,
But hing [hang] *your heads, and bow your crooked*
  crags [necks],
And dresse you all in sackcloth and in rags,
No more to see the Sun, nor fertile fields,
But closely keep you mourning in your bields [shelters],
And for your part the trible [treble] *to you take,*
And when you cry make all your crags to crake [shake],
And shiver when you sing alace for Gall!
Ah if our mourning might thee now recall!

Copy of A. Rutherford's *Plan and Survey of the Town of Perth*. This early 19th-century manuscript copy of Rutherford's map of Perth was appended to the 1774 edition of *The Muses Threnodie* in the National Library of Scotland. The North Inch, where Master Gall probably played his golf, is on the right-hand side. (National Library of Scotland, EMS.s.462)

parish church, providing the course remained in use as a playing field.[3] Haarlem it would seem was exceptional, and generally, at least in the days before areas were specifically set aside for the game, golf was a seasonal activity, with play being dictated as much by the other uses of the course as the leisure time of the players.

In seventeenth-century Scotland it was normal for golfing grounds to be used for many other purposes. Greens, such as that in Perth, were treated as common land where animals might graze. They might also be used as drying grounds for laundry. Recreation was but one use to which these areas might be put, and golf was only one sport among many. The coastal links too had many functions. As early as 1552 the St Andrews Links were set aside for 'golfe, futeball, shuting and all games' (see page 23). Leith Links were a well-known venue for archers, and the Races there were a regular feature of the Scottish sporting and social calendar until they were transferred to Musselburgh in 1816. Musselburgh too is

(see page 23).

ABOVE
Adriaen van de Velde, *Golfers on the Ice near Haarlem*, 1668. This painting shows two of the players wearing kilts. It may be they were Scottish merchants or soldiers who happened to be in the Low Countries. (The National Gallery, London)

an example of links being used as a play ground for all. With so many activities taking place, it is to be wondered if such areas were actually any safer than the streets and kirk yards had been in the past.

Given the evidence for golf on Scotland's eastern coast from Edinburgh and Leith to Aberdeen and Dornoch, it is hardly surprising to find the game was played elsewhere in north-east Scotland in the seventeenth century. One keen golfer who is known to have played at a number of places along this coast was the 1st Marquis of Montrose.

Born James Graham, the 1st Marquis of Montrose is arguably one of the most controversial of seventeenth-century Scots. His long and eventful career as soldier, statesman and politician ended in 1650 when he was hanged as a traitor in the Grassmarket, Edinburgh. As a young man Montrose was a noted sportsman. His prowess as an archer is well known, as he won the prize of the Silver Arrow at St Andrews. The family account books reveal that the Marquis was also a golfer, who played at Arbroath, Montrose and St Andrews in the late 1620s.[4]

In 1628 Montrose went to St Andrews University where his financial affairs were managed by a 'pursemaster', Mr John Lambie. Lambie's detailed accounts provide a remarkable picture of Montrose's life at the University and, in particular, of his recreations. The Marquis's favourite sport was undoubtedly archery, and his room is said to have been hung with bows. He also played golf on the links at St Andrews and Leith, regularly visited the Races at nearby Cupar, hawked, hunted, and also played tennis at Leith.

So fond of golf was Montrose that he played the day before his marriage to 'sweet Mistress Magdalene Carnegie', as his accounts record: 'Item, the nynthe day [9 November 1629] in Montrois, my Lord playing at the golf with the Laird of Lusse, for two golf balls ... 24sh.' Only a few days after the wedding, the Marquis sent to St Andrews for new golfing equipment and repairs to his old clubs: 'Item, the nynteen day to ane boy going to St Andrews for clubs and bals to my Lord ... 32sh. Item, for sax new clubs and dressing som auld clubs, and for balls ... 11 lib. 8sh.'

The accounts mention a St Andrews club-maker, James Pett, by name 'for furnishing my Lord with bows and arrows and clubs that year 7 lib. 8 sh'. Pett is described as a 'bower' in the accounts, indicating that bow-makers were making golf clubs in St Andrews in the 1620s, as they had in 1502 when James IV played at Perth.

Further north, in Banffshire in 1690, James Ogilvie wrote from Boyne to his cousins in Cullen, inviting them to play 'long gouf' on the sea braes near Boyne Castle. This letter would suggest that the cousins met regularly for golf. James Ogilvie left it to the others to choose where they were to play, although he hints that the links at Boyne were better than those near Cullen House, the home of the Earl of Seafield, where his cousins lived. It seems they too had more than one club available, as reference is made to 'your short putting club'. Ogilvie ends with a gentle jibe concerning a game played by the cousins earlier at Eden in Aberdeenshire, which presumably was a sore point with Mr Patrick and his brother: '... we shall see ife ye cannot make better use of a club in this countrey then ye did at Eden.'

March 1629
Item, for balls in the tinnes [tennis] *court of Leith … 16sh.*

Item, for two goffe balls, my Lord going to the goffe ther … 10sh.

Ife Mr. Patrick and you have a mind for a touch at long gouff tomorrow Lett me know this night wher I shall waitt on you with a second, or if yee would do me the honour to come this lenth [length]*, because the* *links ar better, and we shall see ife ye cannot make better use of a club in this countrey then ye did at Eden. this is not that I doubt but ye made good use of your short putting club ther.*[5]

NOTES

1 Henry Adamson: *The Muses Threnodie, or Mirthfull Mournings on the Death of Master Gall* (Edinburgh, 1638).

2 National Archives of Scotland, E21.

3 van Hengel, p. 20.

4 Mark Napier: *Memorials of Montrose and his Times*, Maitland Club (Edinburgh, 1848), vol. 1, pp. 156-201.

5 National Archives of Scotland, GD 248.

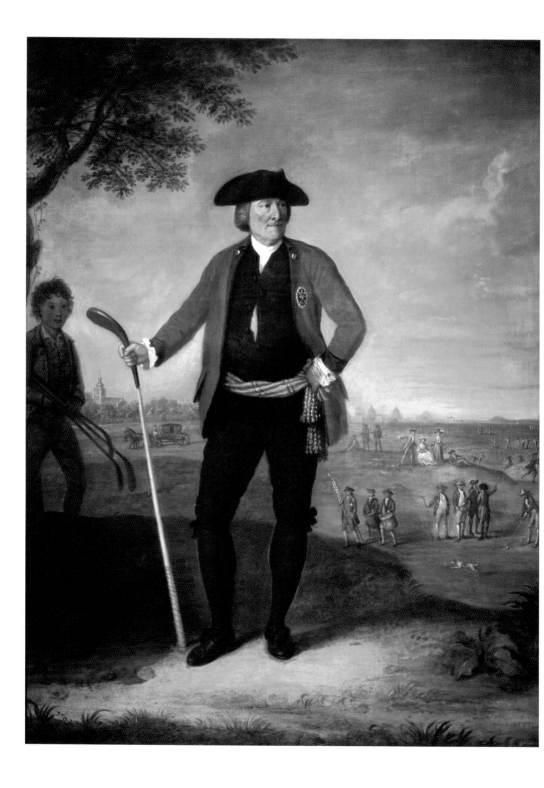

AN EDINBURGH SPORTSMAN

SIR JOHN FOULIS OF RAVELSTON

1686

Sir John Foulis of Ravelston kept a meticulous record of his everyday expenditure in a series of nine pocket-sized account books. Numbers 2 and 3 in the series, covering the years 1684-89, came to the National Library of Scotland in 1936 with the Liston Foulis papers.[1] These account books are the two volumes said to be missing by A. W. C. Hallen in his 1894 edition of Sir John's accounts for the Scottish History Society.[2]

A country gentleman with an estate at Ravelston, then a few miles outside Edinburgh, Sir John was a keen sportsman. The accounts tell of Sir John's life in the country, and in Edinburgh where he spent much time both on business and pleasure. He held the office of Keeper of the Register of Sasines and had his town house in Foster's Wynd. There is much information about Sir John's large family, his friends and acquaintancies, pastimes and recreations. The overall impression is of a conscientious, caring family man, a sociable individual with many friends who participated in a wide range of recreations; above all, Sir John Foulis was a man who enjoyed life.

OPPOSITE

David Allan, *William Inglis*, *c.*1712-1792. *Surgeon and Captain of the Honourable Company of Edinburgh Golfers* [detail]. (Scottish National Portrait Gallery)

This painting shows William Inglis on Leith Links in 1787, some hundred years after Sir John Foulis played there. In the background is the Procession of the Silver Club (see chapter on 'The First Rules of Golf', pages 86-94), for which prize the members of the Company of Gentlemen Golfers competed.

Amusements feature large in the accounts. Sir John enjoyed many of the field sports popular with country gentlemen at the end of the seventeenth century. He hunted hares with hounds, kept greyhounds probably for coursing, and hawked and fished on his estate at Ravelston. We also know that he was a regular bowler at Potterow in Edinburgh, and that while in town he diced and played cards. Gossip with friends in taverns and other meeting places seems to have been a regular indulgence. Sir John also enjoyed horse racing and rarely missed the annual spring race meeting at Leith. He seems to have been somewhat less fond of curling though, as the sport is mentioned only occasionally. Given this range of sporting activities, and the proximity of the links at Leith to Ravelston, it is hardly surprising that Sir John was also a golfer.

Golf seems to have been Sir John's favourite sport and he played regularly at Leith. His accounts do not give a great deal of information as to how the game was played, but they are of value in other ways. They tell us, for example, that a golf ball bought in Leith in the 1680s cost five shillings, and clubs ten shillings. There are also references to different types of clubs, such as 'my play club' and a 'lead scraper club', on 30 January 1686. On that date Sir John had a new head fixed to his lead club and the play club mended for a total of 14 shillings. It has been estimated that clubs lasted on average only ten rounds.[3] Then, as now, golfing equipment was expensive, and even a gentleman of considerable means is seen taking the trouble to have his clubs repaired and renewed.

48

LEFT

30 January 1686
to malcolme to pay for a new head to
a Lead Scraper club[4] *& mending*
my play club 00:14:0
Lent to mrs dunbar 29:0:0
Spent at golf and coatch hyres [coach hires]
and Supper wt [with] *moncreife* [and]
Inglistone etc. 3:15:0

RIGHT

22 December 1686
for a golfe ball the coatchmans chopine eall
[measure of ale], *& lent to* L[ord Clerk]:
Register for a horne to his club
& [to the] *poor folk* 0:8:0
for carieing [carrying] *my clubs* 0:4:0
my Lord register payed our Supper

On 22 December 1686 Sir John made a payment of four shillings 'for carieing my clubs'. Caddies are mentioned in connection with golf from the early sixteenth century. The Marquis of Montrose had employed a boy to carry his clubs in 1628, and Andrew Dickson was named as the future James VII and II's caddy when he played at Leith in 1681. Until at least the eighteenth century, however, a 'caddy' meant a porter or someone who ran errands, and did not specifically refer to a person who carried golf clubs. Bags were not regularly used until the last decade of the nineteenth century, and Sir John's caddy would have simply tucked the clubs under his arm, much as a sporting gun might be carried.

Sir John seems to have enjoyed the social aspect of his sport. His account books regularly record the names of his companions, how much

Extracts from the *Account Books of Sir John Foulis of Ravelston, 1686-89.* (National Library of Scotland, MSS.6153-4)

he wagered on the outcome of a game, and details of the entertainment enjoyed afterwards. The entry on page 49 for 22 December 1686 shows that on this occasion Sir John's golfing companion was Sir George Mackenzie, later Earl of Cromartie. Mackenzie, described here by his office as Lord Clerk Register, paid for supper after the game. The coachman too is not forgotten, and the purchase of his measure of ale is recorded along with a new ball and Sir John's loan to Mackenzie to purchase a 'horne to his club'. Other companions of Sir John's over the years were drawn from the leading political and legal figures of the time, and include Sir John Baird of Newbyth, Sir Archibald Primrose, and Sir Peter Wedderburn of Gosford. Often four or five names might be given, followed by an 'etc', suggesting Foulis was listing a few notables among the company and that a considerable number of golfers had gone out to play that day.

Sir John played his golf entirely during the winter and usually at weekends. In the four months from December 1685 to the end of March 1686, he records eight outings to play on Leith Links, indicating a game about once a fortnight. He may well have played more often, as on several other occasions Sir John spent time with his golfing cronies but does not specify for what activity, if any, they met. The bill for the eight golfing outings came to £21 10 shillings for equipment, wagers, coach hire, and entertainment in the form of food and drink. Unfortunately the accounts often record only total expenditure, and so it is not possible to calculate how much he spent on golfing equipment alone.

Sir John Foulis's account books give the impression of golf as a thoroughly enjoyable recreation far removed from the image of the game as a rowdy and dangerous pastime, as earlier records suggest. There were, however, still risks attached to the sport in the late seventeenth-century as there are today. Writing in his autobiography in 1690, Sir Robert Sibbald, the physician and antiquary, noted in graphic medical detail an unprovoked attack made on him while he was returning home from visiting a patient in Leith.[5]

Ane accident befell me the 16 of October 1690 that as I was coming from Sir Robert Milne his house in Leith, where I had been visiting his Good Brother Mr. Elphiston's wyfe, who had taken physick that day, about four afternoon as I was going down to passe the Ditch to goe to the Links wher I left some Company playing at Goufe & my servant following me, neither he nor I nor the boy adverting I was strucken wt the back of the Club wt much force betwixt the Eyes at the root of the nose, the wound was oblong large, and about half ane inch long it was not half ane inch above the cartilage of the nose, the parts under the right eye was livid, and both the Canthi Majores were swelled I bled much & took a coach & came up, & was a good whyl befor I could want a plaister upon it. It was God his great goodness that neither the Cartilage was cut, nor one of ye Eye putt out for it was done with the sharpe syde of the Club.

NOTES

1 National Library of Scotland, MSS.6153-4.

2 A. W. C. Hallen: *The Account Book of Sir John Foulis of Ravelston, 1671-1707*, Scottish History Society (Edinburgh, 1894).

3 David Hamilton: *Early Golf at St Andrews* (Glasgow, 1986), p. 26.

4 Probably a spooned club with a leaded heel.

5 National Library of Scotland, Adv.MS.33.5.1, pp. 72-73. The original manuscript of Sibbald's autobiography appears to be lost. This copy was made in 1805.

[26 January 1687]

      ... I thought on the playing

1 *at the Golve. I found that, ye most rest most*
upon the right legg for the most part but yet
not too much for as to be exactly perpendi-
cular upon it, which ye will know by the
ballance

2 *ing of your body. 2 I found that the club most*
always move in a circle makeing ane angle of
45 degrees with the

3 *horizon. 3 That the whole turning of your*
body about most be by thrawing the joynts
of your right legg and then when [missing] ...
you most thraw the

      thraw the small of your back so that
the left shoulder will turn a little down wards,
because the body is inclined a little forward,
but ye most beware of raising the on shoulder
higher than the other as to their position in
the body, for

4 *that motion is not convenient for this action. 4*
I found that that in bringing down the club
ye most turn your body as farr about towards
the left following the swinge of the club as it
had been turned before towards the right
hand.

DIARY OF AN EDINBURGH MEDICAL STUDENT

THOMAS KINCAID

1687-88

At about the same time as Sir John Foulis was enjoying his regular social round of golf with his cronies on Leith Links, a young Edinburgh medical student, Thomas Kincaid, was taking the game far more seriously. In his diary, Kincaid analyses and describes the game, and in so doing produces the earliest known written set of golfing instructions.[1]

The son of a surgeon-apothecary, Thomas Kincaid studied medicine in Edinburgh in the mid-1680s. His diary covers only a few months from January 1687 to December 1688; however, this is no ordinary journal of social engagements. Rather, Thomas seems to have meditated, usually in the small hours, on a wide range of subjects, later confiding his 'thoughts' to his diary. So, day after day, the diary begins, 'Today I thought upon …', before Thomas proceeds to write up his myriad reflections in considerable detail. As might be expected, there is much relating to medicine, but the young Thomas seems to have had an enquiring mind with many interests, including theology, literature, politics, music and sport, to name but a few.

OPPOSITE, PICTURE
Paul Sandby's *A View of Bruntsfield Links Looking Towards Edinburgh Castle*, 1746. Bruntsfield Links, then about a mile outside Edinburgh, were a popular golfing ground, probably from the 16th century; but as Sandby's *View* indicates, conditions were not ideal. (The British Museum)

OPPOSITE, TEXT
Extract from *Thomas Kincaid's diary*, 1687-88 (National Library of Scotland, Adv.MSS.32.7.7)

Golf and archery were Thomas Kincaid's main sporting activities, and he makes frequent reference to both. Kincaid's career as an archer is better recorded than his prowess as a golfer, and it is known that in later life he was a member of the Royal Company of Archers and won the Edinburgh Silver Arrow in 1711. The golf instructions in the diary occur in the January and February of 1687, when Kincaid notes regular forays on the links. Like Sir John Foulis, Thomas Kincaid played golf during the winter months. They also shared a preference for Leith Links; however Bruntsfield Links, much nearer to his Edinburgh lodgings than Leith, are mentioned too, and it seems likely he also played there.

Much of what is known of Bruntsfield Links at the time comes from the English artist, Paul Sandby. Sandby was employed in the military drawing department at the Tower of London from 1741, and in 1746 was in Scotland as a draughtsman on the Highland survey commissioned to strengthen the army in Scotland against further Jacobite activities. Sandby's survey drawings, presented to the Board of Ordnance, are now in the British Museum. The view shown on pages 52-53, made during his time in Scotland, depicts Edinburgh Castle perched above the town with Bruntsfield Links in the foreground. A group of figures, possibly soldiers with their caddies, are playing golf. As Sandby's pictures are known for their topographical accuracy, it seems probable he did actually witness a game of golf taking place.

Bruntsfield Links were at the time about a mile outside Edinburgh. They were quarried from at least 1508, and as a result were soon indented with large holes from which the soft, grey sandstone which typifies many of the buildings in the city and Leith, was extracted. The remaining areas were used by the citizens for golf, while the quarries, one of which is visible in Paul Sandby's picture, were utilised as bunkers. The Edinburgh Burgh records indicate the importance attached to the area as a golfing ground, since many of the tacks, or leases, of parts of the links reserve the rights of golfers.[2]

In 1723 the lease to John Paterson to graze his cattle on the links reserved the right to play golf, to walk on the links, to dry clothes in the bushes, to muster troops, and to use the springs of water. The records

also reveal the poor condition of the links for golf, with descriptions of rocky areas, bogs, gorse and whin. The area was not cleared until the mid-eighteenth century.[3] Given the condition of Bruntsfield Links, it is perhaps understandable that, so often, Kincaid and other residents of Edinburgh seem to have preferred to play at nearby Leith.

Despite the poor condition of the links at Bruntsfield, there is little doubt that they were regularly used for golf, as Allan Ramsay's *Elegy on Maggy Johnston Who died Anno 1711* testifies.[4] Maggy Johnston kept a tavern at the edge of Bruntsfield Links, which Ramsay tells us was so popular that, 'Of Customers she had a Bang [a great number]; / For Lairds and Souters [commoners] a[ll] did gang / *To drink bedeen*, / The Barn and Yard was aft sae thrang [crowded], / *We took the Green*'. Ramsay continues mournfully, 'Whan we were weary'd at the Gouff / Then MAGGY JOHNSTON's was our Houff [tavern]; / Now a[ll] our Game-sters [players] may sit douff [melancholy], / *Wi' Hearts like Lead*, / Death wi' his Rung rax'd her a Youff [Death with his stick reached her a blow], / *And sae she died*'.

Gordon Story's *Bruntsfield Golf Tavern*. (Central Library, Edinburgh)

55

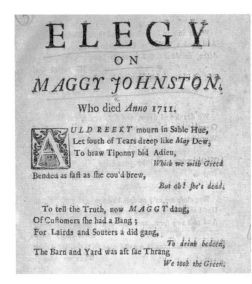

ELEGY
ON
MAGGY JOHNSTON,
Who died *Anno* 1711.

*A*ULD REEKY mourn in Sable Hue,
Let fouth of Tears dreep like *May* Dew;
To braw Tiponny bid Adieu,
                    Which we with Greed
Bended as faft as fhe cou'd brew,
                              But ah! fhe's dead,

To tell the Truth, now *MAGGY* dang,
Of Cuftomers fhe had a Bang ;
For Lairds and Souters a did gang,
                              To drink bedeen;
The Barn and Yard was aft fae Thrang
                              We took the Green;

Allan Ramsay, *Elegy on Maggy Johnston Who died Anno 1711* (Edinburgh, 1718), p. 1. Here, Allan Ramsay tells of large numbers of golfers on Bruntsfield Links. (National Library of Scotland, F.5.b.9)

Ramsay's lament for Maggy Johnston may make reference to golf on Bruntsfield Links, but it is to Thomas Kincaid's diary we must turn for a detailed set of instructions on how the game should be played. The extracts quoted from the diary form only a fraction of his thoughts on golf, yet they alone indicate how he analyses his game in minute detail down to the positioning of the body, the grip on the club, and the angle of swing. On 26 January 1687 he describes and analyses his very flat swing. This is appropriate to the clubs of the time, which were generally long and heavy by modern standards.

Kincaid was equally adamant about the construction of his golfing equipment. Concerning golf clubs, he wrote: 'The shaft of your club most be made of hazell. Your club most be almost straight that is the head most make a verie obtuse angle with the shaft, and it most bend as much at the handle as it does at the wooping [the grip], being verie supple and both long and great.' No hazel-shafted clubs have as yet been discovered. All known seventeenth-century wooden clubs are ash, with the exception of a few lead clubs with alder shafts.

Kincaid records some purchases of golfing equipment. During early February 1687 he was ill, but by the 8th of the month, when he received a visit from his friend and golfing companion Henry Legatt, he felt well enough to rise from his sick bed and took the coach to Leith. There Legatt 'bought a club in Captain Foster's', and later Kincaid bought three balls for 14 shillings.

> Hen: Legatt came in and desired me to go out to the golve. I putt on my cloths, and went to him he bought a club at Captain Foster's we went down to Leith In a Coach which was 10 shill[ings] we played till 5 I bought three balls 14 shill[ings] we went to Captain Brown's where we settled waiting on the coach but could not gett it …. I was exceeding seek.

In spite of his stringent requirements for golfing equipment, Kincaid attempted his own repairs. On 25 January 1687 he notes: 'I glewed the club head … after dinner I took out the plains and made a little skelpe [splinter] to putt on the club. I took of the piece that was joynd to the old shaft. I glewed too that skelpe.'

A variety of golf balls seem to have been available. Kincaid recommends that

> … your balls most be of a middle size nither too big nor too little, and then the heivier it is in respect of its bigness it is still the better. It most be of thick and hard leather not with pores or grains or that will let a pin easily passe throughe it especially at the soft end.

As well as attempting his own club repairs, Kincaid experimented with golf balls, colouring 'a golve ball with white lead'. Among the failings of the featherie ball was that it was porous and easily lost its shape and resilience in wet weather. Colouring the ball with white lead served the dual purpose of making the ball more conspicuous and less liable to take in water.

Also of interest are Kincaid's thoughts on what appears to be an early handicap system:

God: and wrott this till 9. I found that I do not
have a book wherein I might writt down previously all things you think remarkable, with the
of the author and place where you may find it
and then when you have leasure you may reade
all over and digest them into order and will the
down in another book. I read some of Barclay
vergia, till 12: after dinner I went out to the Golf
lisn: Logall I found that the only way of playing
at the Golfe is to stand as youre at fencing with
small sword bending yeur legs a little and hold..
muscles of your legs and back and armes: ope the
bent or fist or staffe: and not at all slackning
in the time you are bringing down the stroak b
you readily doe,) The ball most be straight before
foeall, a little towards the left foot: your left foot
stand but a little before the right, or rather it most
with it, and at a convenient distance from it, you
most to the right foot: but all the turning about of
body most be only at the small of your back and
tilt upon your legs holding them as stiff as you can, the
inclint your body a little forward, from the small of
and upwards for being all the strenth of the stroake is
huing of the body in turning about, then certainly

... I thought upon the question whither it is better in giveing advantadge in gameing to make the game equal and the stakes unequal, or to make the stakes equal and give some advantadge in the game; as at the golve whither it is better to give a man two holes of three, laying equal stakes, or to lay three stakes to his on and equal for so much every hole.

He concludes here that 'with these that are worst gamesters than yourselfe, make always the game depend upon moe hazards than on[e], and the moe the better; but with these that are better gamesters make always the game to depend only upon on[e] hazard'.

The final section on golf in the diary takes the form of a poem. Again, this seems to be a 'first' for Kincaid. Other seventeenth-century poems, including Henry Adamson's *The Muses Threnodie* of 1638, mention golf (see pages 39-41), but this may well be the first poem entirely devoted to golf. On 9 February 1687 Kincaid's thoughts seem to have been darting from one subject to another in typical fashion before he gathered them together and wrote:

[20 January 1687]

  ... after dinner I went out to the Golve with Hen: Legatt I found that the only way of playing

1 *at the Golve is to stand as you do at fenceing with the small sword bending your legs a little and holding the muscles of your legs*

and back and armes exceeding bent or fixt or stiffe and not at all slackning them in the time you are bringing down the stroak (which

2 *you readily doe,) the ball most be straight before your*

3 *breast, a little towards the left foot 3 your left foot most stand but a little before the right, or rather it most be even*

4 *with it, and at a convenient distance from it, 4 ye most lean*

5 *most to the right foot, 5 but all the turning about of your body most be only ... upon your legs holding them as stiff as ye can ...*

59

9 Wed. I rose at 7. I thought upon the method of pathologie, and on playing at the golve .... I digested the rules of playing at the golve into verse thus.

> Gripe fast stand with your left leg first not farr
> Incline your back and shoulders but beware
> You raise them not when back the club you bring
> Make all the motion with your bodies swinge
> And shoulders, holding still the muscles bent
> Play slowly first till you the way have learnt
> At such lenth hold the club as fitts your strenth
> The lighter head requires the longer lenth
> That circle wherein moves your club and hands
> At forty five degrees from th[e] horizon stands
> What at on[e] stroak to effectuat you dispaire
> Seek only 'gainst the nixt it to prepare.

Elsewhere in the diary, Kincaid describes his method as 'the only way of playing at the golve'. Whether or not other golfers agreed with him is not known, as no comparable series of instructions for this time exists. What can be said, however, is that in writing down his 'thoughts' on golf, Thomas Kincaid anticipated the first published golfing poem, Thomas Mathison's *The Goff* of 1743, by over 50 years (see pages 77-81), and the first printed book of golf instruction, H. B. Farnie's *The Golfer's Manual, By a Keen Hand*, published in 1857, by 170 years.

NOTES

1 Diary of Thomas Kincaid, 1687-88 (National Library of Scotland, Adv.MS.32.7.7). For a more detailed discussion of Thomas Kincaid's diary, see Henry W. Meikie: 'An Edinburgh Diary', in *Book of the Old Edinburgh Club* (Edinburgh, 1949), vol. 27, pp. 111-54.

2 Extracts from the Records of the Burgh of Edinburgh 1701-18, Scottish Burgh Record Society (London, 1967), pp. 62, 215.

3 C. E. S. Chambers: 'Early Golf at Bruntsfield and Leith', in *Book of the Old Edinburgh Club* (Edinburgh, 1932), vol. 18, pp. 1-10.

4 Allan Ramsay, *Elegy on Maggy Johnston Who died Anno 1711* (Edinburgh, 1718), pp. 1-4.

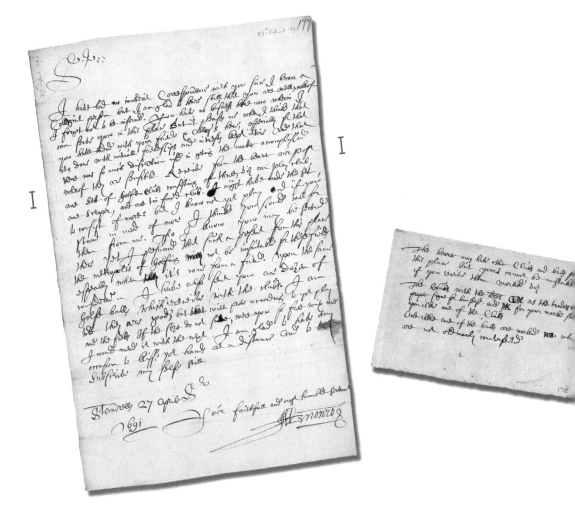

Receive from the bearer our post ane Sett of Golfe-Clubs consisting of three, viz. an play club,[1] ane Scraper,[2] and ane tin fac'd club.[3] I might have made the set to consist of more: but I know not your play and if you stand in need of more I think you should call for them from me. Tho I know you may be served thear yet I presumed

that such a present from this place the metropolis of Golfing may not be unsuitable for these fields especially when it's come from a friend. Upon the same consideration I have also sent you ane Dozen of Golfe balls which receive with the clubs. I am told they are good, but that will prove according to your play and the fields. If the size

do not suite, were you so free with me I would mend it with the next. I am glad to have any occasion to kiss your hands at a distance And to Subscribe my selfe still

Sir
Your faithfull and most
humble servant
Al. Monro
St Andrews 27 April 1691

'THE METROPOLIS
OF GOLFING'

ST ANDREWS
1691-1716

The Mackenzie of Delvine Papers, now in the National Library of Scotland, have a curious history. At some point, probably in the early nineteenth century, the door of the cupboard in which they had been placed was papered over. The papers were forgotten about and were only discovered accidentally by the butler at Delvine House, near Dunkeld in Perthshire, in 1918. These are the papers of a family of lawyers, at least one of whom was a golfer.[4]

John Mackenzie was the third son of Sir Kenneth Mackenzie, the 1st Baronet of Coul. Admitted to the Faculty of Advocates in 1681, his legal career soon prospered, and he rose to become one of the Principal Clerks of Session in 1686. On the proceeds of his legal practice, Mackenzie purchased an estate at King's Cramond near Edinburgh in 1697. In 1705 he followed this with the purchase of the larger property of Delvine in Perthshire. The family continued to prosper for some time and in the early nineteenth century John Mackenzie's grandson was created Baronet of Delvine.

OPPOSITE, LEFT
Letter of Alexander Monro to John Mackenzie of Delvine, 27 April 1691. Monro's letter to his friend John Mackenzie informed him that he had despatched to him a gift of 'ane Sett of Golfe-Clubs ... from this place the metropolis of Golfing'. (NLS, MS.1393, ff.177-178)

OPPOSITE, RIGHT
The bearer may have other Clubs and balls from this place but yours cannot be mistaken if you receive them marked viz.

The Clubs with the Lres [letters] G.M. as the tradesmans proper signe for himselfe, and JMK for your mark stamped upon ilke ane of the Clubs ....
And ilke ane of the balls are marked W.B. which are not ordinarily counterfeited.

63

Golfers on the Links at St Andrews, c.1740 [detail]. This painting, by an unknown artist, may be the earliest picture to show golf being played in Britain. (Reproduced by kind permission of The Royal and Ancient Golf Club, St Andrews)

On 27 April 1691 John Mackenzie received a letter from his friend, Alexander Monro, then a Regent at St Andrews University, informing him that he had despatched to him by bearer 'ane Sett of Golfe-Clubs'.[5]

Like his friend, John Mackenzie, Alexander Monro had also begun his career in the legal profession, in his case as a Writer in Edinburgh. This letter, and the 20 or so others in the collection written by him to John Mackenzie between 1688 and 1697, suggest that they had known each other in Edinburgh legal circles and become firm friends. When he wrote in the spring of 1691 Monro had recently taken up the position of Regent and Professor of Philosophy at St Andrews University. He was to become Provost or Principal of St Salvator's College, St Andrews, before his death in 1697. Monro's business interests, and later his academic appointments, may have taken him from Edinburgh after 1688, but the letters indicate that he was determined not to lose touch with his friends. In a letter of May 1688 he writes, 'I always mynd my friends and sometimes drink their health and particularly yours'.[6] What better

64

way to maintain a friendship than to send a present of a set of golf clubs and balls from 'the metropolis of Golfing'?

Monro's gift was clearly a present from one golfer to another, although as they had not met for some time he apologised in case the clubs and balls were not suitable. 'I might have made the set to consist of more but I know not your play.' Three different clubs are mentioned: 'an play club, ane scraper, and ane tin fac'd club.' Apparently others were available in St Andrews at the time as, Monro acknowledged, they were also in Edinburgh. Golf balls too were sent by the bearer, and we are told that these could be changed if they proved inappropriate either for Mackenzie's style of play or his chosen course.

The letter indicates that there was a regular traffic in golfing equipment between St Andrews and Edinburgh during the late seventeenth century. So concerned was Munro about possible confusion with other golfing items carried by the bearer, or indeed theft, that he felt it necessary to advise his friend that the distinguishing marks of the tradesman's and Mackenzie's initials had been stamped on both the clubs and balls.

In addition to correspondence with old and valued friends such as Alexander Monro, John Mackenzie of Delvine's papers include accounts accompanied by reports in the form of a series of letters from James Morice, an employee engaged to help with the upbringing of Mackenzie's large family of 15 children by his three wives.[7]

James Morice was employed by John Mackenzie between 1707 and 1716 as tutor or governor to three of his sons: Alexander, born in 1695, and the twins Kenneth and Thomas, born in 1699. John Mackenzie's family seems to have been too large to have all lived together in the one house, and when Morice was first employed as tutor the twins were staying with him at Craigie, a village a few miles from Delvine. His pupils were then quite young, and Morice reports, 'my Lads have not yet begun as yet to write'.

Kenneth and Thomas joined their older brother, Alexander, at St Andrews University in 1711, and the letters suggest that James Morice did not accompany them. A letter home from Alexander indicates that this arrangement was not satis-factory as regards the twins' education; he writes to his father giving a well-worn excuse: 'The true reason that they [Kenneth and Thomas] are so idle is that they are the best scholars in their class.' By the start of the 1712-13 session, however, James Morice had resumed his charge, over-

Letter of James Morice to John Mackenzie, 26 November 1712. In this letter to his employer, James Morice enquires how often his charges are to be allowed to play golf. (National Library of Scotland, MS.1400, f.152)

66

seeing the boys' education, accommodation, and even their recreations.

Their tutor's discipline seems to have had the desired effect, and in September 1713 Kenneth wrote home: 'By being kept close at our studies we find that now to be an easy diversion, which which [*sic*] was wont to be a fashious [tedious] task.' Life as a student under James Morice was not all work, and in his first letter from St Andrews to John Mackenzie he enquires, 'what you allow on ye young Gentlemen weekly for yr diversion at the golf'. John Mackenzie is known to have been a golfer himself, and clearly approved of the recreation, and so the answer is hardly surprising: 'When the weather is fair I allow the Twins to go to the golf twice a week according to your order.' Morice's accounts indicate that the boys took full advantage of this instruction and more as, save when exams loomed, they might be found on the links as often as three times a week.

The main interest of the accounts lies in the information they give of golfing equipment. Balls and clubs seem to have been purchased locally, and Henry Mills, club-maker in St Andrews, is mentioned by name. Of the three boys, Alexander was probably the best golfer. He had three clubs in his set, each costing twelve shillings. The twins at first had one club each worth ten shillings; later their clubs cost twelve shillings each. This may have been because they became more skilful, or merely because they were older. There is a record of the purchase of an iron club for the twins to share which cost one pound and four shillings. Parts of

Letter of James Morice to John Mackenzie, 2 June 1713. In a postscript to this letter to his employer, James Morice notes: 'Henry Mill ye Club- maker's receipt is herein enclosed together wit ye accompt ....' Unfortunately the receipt has not survi- ved. (National Library of Scotland, MS.1400, f. 167)

[1714]

Accompt of Disbursements for K[enneth] and Th[omas] Mackenzies

	£	sh	d
Ballance of the last year's accompt sent over Novr. 1714 due to me was	18:07:00		
1 Nov. to yr [their] Regent Mr. Vilant 2 Guineas	25:16:00		
7 to ye poor 2sh / 8 / for 2 dozen pens 2sh	00:04:00		
11 for an iron club to ythm [them]	01:04:00		
14 to the poor 2sh / 17 / for soling Th[omas]'s shoos 7sh 6d	00:09:06		
21 to ye poor 2sh 6d / 25 / for 13 balls to ythm [them] ilk 4sh 3d	01:05:06		

the club might be purchased separately: a club-head cost four shillings or six shillings, a new shaft four shillings, and 'a horn to Thomas's club' was two shillings. On average, clubs lasted about ten rounds, but new balls had to be bought for each game. Balls too came in varying sizes and qualities. Alexander's balls cost four shillings each, but the twins never progressed beyond the two-shilling balls.[8]

The annual expenditure for the three boys on golf, as recorded by Morice, has been calculated as being greater than that for their tuition.[9] Between November 1712 and February 1713, when the boys were playing at least twice a week, Morice spent £17 13 shillings on golfing equipment. Sir John Foulis, who played about once a fortnight on Leith Links in the 1680s, spent £21 on golf in four months in the winter of 1686. As well as clubs and balls, his total bill included expenditure on wagers, coach-hire, and post-match entertainment.[10]

Alexander left University in 1713 and became a lawyer, being admitted a Writer to the Signet in 1714. In 1718 he followed his father as one of the Principal Clerks of Session, succeeding to Delvine in 1731. Of the twins, Kenneth left St Andrews in 1716 and continued his studies at Leyden. He returned to Scotland and was admitted to the Faculty of Advocates in 1718. He became Professor of Civil Law at Edinburgh University and died in 1756. Thomas's fate was not so happy. The letters suggest he was sickly with a recurring cough. He died in 1720, possibly from pulmonary consumption, only four years after he graduated.

James Melville's diary showed golf was played by students at St Andrews in 1574, and Bishop Hamilton's Acknowledgement indicated the game was popular at least as early as 1552 (see page 23). In 1642 sport was sanctioned at St Andrews University by a Report of the University Commissioners which stated that 'Recreations are necessary'. The Report went on to state that only 'laufull exercises, as gouffe, archery, and other of that kind, which are harmeles and do exercise the body' were permitted, and specifically decreed 'there be no carding, dyceing, amongst the students, or exercises of that kynd'.[11]

The Delvine papers indicate that in the early eighteenth century, as in the time of James Melville over a hundred years before, golf was

OPPOSITE
Accounts of James Morice, November 1714. James Morice's accounts include payments for golfing equipment. (National Library of Scotland, MS.1400, f.253)

69

popular at St Andrews with both students and staff. Alexander Monro's letter of 1691 shows that even senior academics indulged, and in 1713 Morice relates how 'since the days become longer, the Masters of the University are found out at the golf in the afternoon'. John Mackenzie sanctioned the quite considerable expenditure on golf gladly, and from the importance he attached to the game it would seem that he considered it to be no mere recreation, but an accomplishment which would stand his sons in good stead throughout their professional lives.

NOTES

1   A driving wood.

2   A lofting wood.

3   Probably an iron club.

4   National Library of Scotland, MSS.1101-1530. See also W. K. Dickson: 'Letters to John Mackenzie of Delvine, Advocate ... 1690-1698', in *Miscellany of the Scottish History Society* (1933), vol. V, pp. 197-290.

5   National Library of Scotland, MS.1393, ff.177-178.

6   National Library of Scotland, MS.1393, f.170.

7   National Library of Scotland, MS.1400. For a more detailed discussion of these papers, see William Croft Dickinson: *Two Students at St Andrews, 1711-16* (Edinburgh, 1952).

8   The Mackenzie boys' expenses at St Andrews are considered in detail in David Hamilton: *St Andrews Golf* (Glasgow, 1986).

9   Hamilton: *St Andrews Golf*.

10   See chapter on Sir John Foulis of Ravelston, pp. 47-51.

11   St Andrews University Commissioners' Reports, 206.

GLOTTA
AN EYE-WITNESS
ACCOUNT

GLASGOW

1721

Although most early Scottish golf took place on the east coast, the game was known in Glasgow from at least 1589, when the Kirk Session issued a fierce lambast against ball and stick games, decreeing that there be 'no golf, carrict, [or] shinnie [variants of shinty] in the High or the Black-friars Yards, Sunday or weekday'.[1] In banning these games entirely from certain areas, the Church in Glasgow took a different attitude towards golf from that of most other Kirk Sessions: parish records elsewhere, from Perth and Stirling to Banff and Cullen, were generally concerned with Sunday observance and forbade golf on the Sabbath or merely 'in tyme of sermonis' (see chapter, 'The "Unproffitable" Sport', pages 1-11). Given that the game in the street must have been extremely dangerous and a nuisance to passers-by, Glasgow Kirk Session's decree shows commendable concern for public safety.

The then relatively small town of Glasgow had no coastal links for the recreation of its citizens, and the area of common land on the north bank of the Clyde, known as Glasgow Green, was popular for outdoor activities. The Green has had a variety of functions over the centuries: horses and cattle have grazed there during the summer months; crops of grass were grown for sale; there were also orchards, vegetable gardens, and flower beds laid out between paths and trees made it a pleasant place to stroll. In addition, the Green was popular for games and pastimes, one of which was golf. The records of Glasgow Golf Club indicate that they played on the Green from at least 1787 when their surviving minute books start.

Thro' flow'ry Vallies, and enamel'd Meads,
The hastening Flood at length to Glasgow speeds
Its Northern Bank a lovely Green displays,
Whose e'ery Prospect fresh Delights conveys.

THE Muse would sing, when Glasgow she surveys,
But Glasgow's Beauty shall outlast her lays.
Tho' small in Compass, not the lest in Fame,
She boasts her lofty Tow'rs, and antient Name.

While the accounts of the Earls of Annandale record payments for golf clubs and balls for the young Earl William and his brother while at Glasgow Grammar School in 1674,[2] it is impossible to estimate how much golf was played in seventeenth-century Glasgow. In 1642, however, Glasgow University, like St Andrews University in the same year, gave its approval to the game when it pronounced that 'the scholars be excerised in lawful games such as Gouffe, Archerie, and the lyk'.[3] It seems probable that the students took advantage of this excuse to escape from their studies, and in 1721 one of them wrote what may well be the earliest surviving eye-witness account of a game of golf in Scotland.

Little is known about James Arbuckle: he is thought to have been born in Ireland in 1700, and was a friend of the poet Allan Ramsay who himself alluded to golf in his poems, *Health* and *Elegy on the Death of Maggy Johnston* (see page 55). By the time *Glotta* was published in 1721, Arbuckle had already had some limited success as a poet, but it is for *Glotta* he is chiefly known. The poem gives a detailed description of the course of the River Clyde (the 'Glotta' of the title), and in doing so, records a game of golf on Glasgow Green.[4]

> The hastening Flood at length to *Glasgow* speeds.
> Its *Northern* Bank a lovely Green displays,
> Whose e'ery Prospect fresh Delights conveys.
>
> In *Winter* too, when hoary Frosts o'erspread,
> The verdant *Turf*, and naked lay the Mead,
> The vig'rous Youth commence the sportive War,
> And arm'd with Lead, their jointed Clubs prepare;

OPPOSITE, PICTURE
J. Brooks, *The Glasgow Bridges and Merchants' Tower*, 1806. This watercolour depicts some of the numerous activities which took place on Glasgow Green: children play, dogs frisk, and the gentry stroll, while, close at hand, milkmaids and washer-women toil. (Glasgow City Council [museums])

OPPOSITE, TEXT
Extract from James Arbuckle's *Glotta*, Glasgow, 1721. (National Library of Scotland, Jac.V.7/2.1[4])

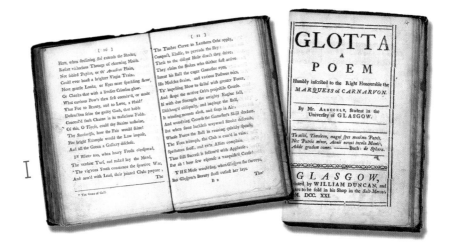

James Arbuckle,
Glotta (Glasgow,
1721). In his poem
eulogising the River
Clyde, James
Arbuckle records a
game of golf on
Glasgow Green.
(National Library
of Scotland,
Jac.V.7/2.1[4])

The Timber Curve to Leathern Orbs apply,
Compact, Elastic, to pervade the Sky:
These to the distant Hole direct they drive;
They claim the Stakes who thither first arrive.
Intent his Ball the eager Gamester eyes,
His Muscles strains, and various Postures tries,
Th' impelling Blow to strike with greater Force,
And shape the motive Orb's projectile Course.
If with due Strength the weighty Engine fall,
Discharg'd obliquely, and impinge the Ball,

It winding mounts aloft, and sings in Air;
And wond'ring Crowds the Gamester's Skill declare.
But when some luckless wayward Stroke descends,
Whose Force the Ball in running quickly spends,
The Foes triumph, the Club is curs'd in vain;
Spectators scoff, and ev'n Allies complain.
Thus still Success is follow'd with Applause;
But ah! how few espouse a vanquish'd Cause!

Only a short section of *Glotta* is devoted to Glasgow Green, which Arbuckle describes as an area of land given over to recreation, 'Whose e'ery Prospect fresh Delights conveys'. According to the poem the Green was popular for an evening stroll: 'Here, when declining Sol extends the shades, / Resort victorious Throngs of charming Maids.' Arbuckle adds to the picturesque scene by informing the reader that the young ladies were dressed in plaids.

Others have given a less romanticised picture of Glasgow Green at the time. James Colville, writing in *The Glasgow Golf Club* (Glasgow, 1907), bemoans the conditions in Arbuckle's time. On his Green, golfers would have had to contend with 'the daily accumulating filth washed down to the Clyde from the Gallowgate, the skinners' yards, redolent of tan, tripe, tallow, and tharm [gut]'. The area was also liable to flooding, leading to deep cart tracks which must have led to many an erratic bounce.

But this is to detract from Arbuckle's scene. Into his idyllic gathering he introduces a group of winter golfers, and then 'The vig'rous Youth commence the sportive War'. We are not told who the players were, and are left to speculate as to whether they were Arbuckle's fellow students at the University. Arbuckle then proceeds to describe the players' expensive golfing equipment consisting of lead, 'jointed', clubs and 'Compact, Elastic', leather (probably featherie) balls, in what must have been a game

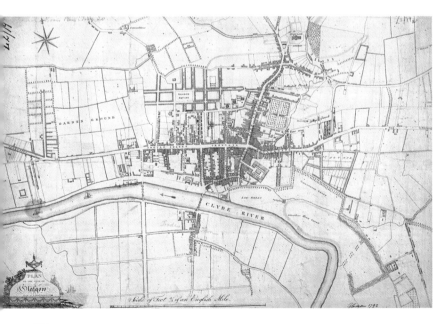

Plan of the City of Glasgow, Board of Ordnance, 1792. This late 18th-century plan of Glasgow, made for the Board of Ordnance, shows the Low Green and High Green alongside the River Clyde. The Washing House, the Herds' House and the Slaughter House are all marked. (National Library of Scotland, Z2/79a)

between quite wealthy players. This was a game of match-play rather than stroke-play, and 'Allies' are mentioned, indicating a foursome.

David Hamilton suggests that James Arbuckle was not a golfer himself, as he seems to consider the game to be one of strength rather than timing, and states that the first player to reach the hole would win the 'stakes'. Perhaps Arbuckle identified more with the excited crowd of clearly knowledgeable spectators than with the players. Be that as it may, his poem has provided us with an important, detailed, account of the way golf was played in the early eighteenth century.

NOTES

1 James Colville: *The Glasgow Golf Club* (Glasgow, 1907), p. 1.

2 Sir William Fraser: *The Annandale Family Book of the Johnstones, Earls and Marquises of Annandale* (Edinburgh, 1894), p. ccliii.

3 Maitland Club, 72 (Glasgow, 1854), vol. 2, p. 466.

4 For a more detailed discussion of James Arbuckle's *Glotta*, see David Hamilton: *Early Golf in Glasgow, 1587-1787* (Oxford, 1985).

THE GOFF

EDINBURGH

1743

Thomas Mathison's mock-heroic epic poem *The Goff*, published in Edinburgh in 1743, is almost certainly the first printed book devoted entirely to golf. The author was born in 1720, the son of an Edinburgh merchant. As a young man he worked as a lawyer in the city, but his career changed direction when he was ordained in 1750. He was appointed Minister of Brechin in 1754 where he remained until his early death in 1760 some six years later. Although he is not known to have written anything else on golf, this poem seems to have arisen out of his love of the game.

The Goff is a poem in three cantos, each over a hundred lines in length, which tells of a game of golf played on Leith Links. These links, where Sir John Foulis and Thomas Kincaid played in the 1680s, are glowingly described as 'that fam'd field, on *Fortha's* sounding shore. / Here, *Caledonian* Chiefs for health resort, / Confirm their sinews by the manly sport'. The first edition (shown here), and the second edition of 1763, give only the initials of the '*Caledonian* Chiefs', the implication being that these were important figures in Edinburgh society needing no further identification to their contemporaries. The third edition, published in 1793, gives the names in full. The poem lists the following golfers:

> Macdonald and unmatc'd Dalrymple ply
> Their pond'rous weapons, and the green defy;
> Rattray for skill, and Corse for strength renown'd,
> Stewart and Lesly beat the sandy ground,

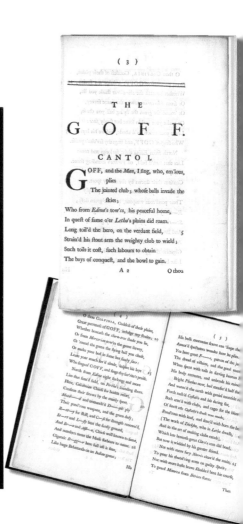

Goff, and the Man, I sing, who, em'lous,[1] plies,
The jointed club; whose balls invade the skies;
Who from Edina's [Edinburgh's] tow'rs, his
    peaceful home,
In quest of fame o'er Letha's [Leith's] plains did
    roam.
Long toil'd the hero, on the verdant field,
Strain'd his stout arm the weighty club to wield;
Such toils it cost, such labours to obtain
The bays of conquest, and the bowl to gain.

O thou GOLFINIA, Goddess of these plains,
Great Patroness of GOFF, indulge my strains;
Whether beneath the thorn-tree shade you lie,
Or from Mercerian tow'rs the game survey,
Or, round the green the flying ball you chase,
Or make your bed in some hot sandy face:
Leave your much lov'd abode, inspire his lays
Who sings of GOFF, and sings thy fav'rit's praise.

North from Edina eight furlongs and more,
Lies that fam'd field, on Fortha's sounding shore.
Here, Caledonian Chiefs for health resort,
Confirm their sinews by the manly sport.

And Brown and Alston, Chiefs well known to fame,
And numbers more the Muse forbears to name.

Most of these players, many of whom were celebrated lawyers and judges, are known to have been among the first members of the Company of Gentlemen Golfers. Among those named are Lord President Forbes, Lord Drummore and Sir Alexander Macdonald. Although the poem shows that these golfers knew each other well and played together regularly, there is no indication that they belonged to a Golf Club at the time of the poem.

Lord President Forbes was an eminent Scottish lawyer and politician described in the anonymous pamphlet *Memoirs of Duncan Forbes of Culloden* (probably published in 1748) as 'a man of such abilities, as would have enabled him to make a bright figure in any station of life'.[2] In spite of the burdens of work, Duncan Forbes's *Memoirs* indicate his legal duties do not seem to have prevented him from playing a regular round of golf.

While Lord Advocate, the *Memoirs* relate that 'during the time of the summer session at Edinburgh, [Forbes] went out every Saturday to Stonie-hill, and … except the time he devoted to hearing sermon, tasted the pleasures of a country life till the Monday that he came to Leith, and there played at the golf'. Forbes also played at Musselburgh. In 1728 he wrote to his brother from Stoneyhill:

This Day after a Very hard Pull I Got the better of My Son
at the Gouf in Musselburgh Links, if he was as Good at any
Other thing as he is at that there might be some hopes of him.

OPPOSITE, LEFT Jeremiah Davison, *Duncan Forbes of Culloden* [detail]. (Scottish National Portrait Gallery)

OPPOSITE, RIGHT: ILLUSTRATION AND TEXT Thomas Mathison, *The Goff: An Heroi-Comical Poem* (Edinburgh, 1743). (National Library of Scotland, RB.s.1405)

An intriguing record of Duncan Forbes's game has survived in the *Memoirs*:

He discoverd a dissatisfaction with such as played carelessly, and never seemed better pleased than when his antagonists exerted themselves against him. He struck the ball full, and having a nervous arm upon a well-pois'd body, he generally drove very far; when nigh the hole, he tipped with so much caution and circumspection that even a lesson might be learned from him in his innocent amusements.

Later, when deeply embroiled in the after-math of the Jacobite Rising of 1745, Forbes had less time for golf; in 1746 he lamented this in a letter to his cousin, William Forbes:

I long to hear what has become of all my golf companions, Particularly whether John Rattray is come back … for I have not for these five months seen anyone that could give me the least satisfaction to my anxiety to know.

John Rattray was the 'Surgeon Rattray' of *The Goff*. He won the City of Edinburgh's competition for the Silver Club in 1744 and 1745 and was the first Captain of the Company of Gentlemen Gofers. (For more information on John Rattray and a detailed discussion of the competition for the Silver Club, see chapter on 'The First "Rules of Golf"'.)

To return to *The Goff*, having set the scene on Leith Links, Mathison then introduces his main protagonists: two keen young golfers, identified in the poem only as 'Castalio' and 'Pygmalion'. He writes:

Bright *Phoebus* now, had measur'd half the day
And warm'd the earth with genial noon-tide ray:
Forth rush'd *Castalio* and his daring foe,
Both arm'd with clubs, and eager for the blow.[3]

The two players were accompanied by 'tattered Irus, who their armour bears'. He acted as caddy to them both and also prepared their tees. Mathison records that he 'Upon the green two little pyr'mids rears; / On these they place two balls with careful eye'. His duties at the tee performed, Irus seems to have gone on ahead to mark where the balls landed. In the days of unprepared courses, a fore-caddy was probably much in demand.

80

The poem records in some detail the progress of the match at all of the five named holes of the course at Leith: the Thorn-tree hole, the Braehead hole, the Sawmill hole, the North Mid-hole, and the South Mid-hole. A match might have consisted of two, three, four, or even five rounds of the course. In this case, there were four rounds, and 20 holes were played. The match had been started under the noon sun, but by the time the last hole, which decided the match, was reached, 'Declining *Sol* with milder beams invades / The *Scotian* fields, and lengthens out the shades'.

Golf courses of the time, and indeed much later, did not have a set number of holes and usually had far fewer than today's standard 18, the exception being St Andrews where there were 22 holes when the Royal and Ancient was formed. The course was shortened in 1750 to 20 holes. Later, it was reduced to 18.

As in James Arbuckle's description of Glasgow golf in his *Glotta* of 1721, the equipment is expensive. Clubs are said to be 'jointed' and the balls are featheries. Mathison gives a graphic description of the making of a featherie ball. They are

> The work of *Bobson*; who with matchless art
> Shapes the firm hide, connecting ev'ry part …
> And thro' the eylet drives the downy tide;
> Crowds urging crowds the forceful brogue impels,
> The feathers harden and the leather swells;
> He crams and sweats, yet crams and urges more,
> Til scarce the turgid globe contains its store.

It is interesting to note that '*Bobson*', probably a contraction of 'Robertson', was a St Andrews ball-maker, and the implication is that although golf balls were made in Leith at the time, the most prized balls came from St Andrews.

We are told less about the making of the clubs used for the match than the balls. Reference is made to Andrew Dickson of Leith, one of the leading club-makers of the time:

Reproductions of
18th-century golf
clubs. This set of
reproduction clubs
includes a play club,
long spoon, short
spoon, putter, heavy
square toe iron, and
a light 'driving' iron.
(Bob Gowland Inter-
national Brokers)

Of finest ash *Castalio's* shaft was made
Pond'rous with lead and fenc'd with horn the head,
The work of *Dickson* who in *Letha* dwells
(And in the art of making clubs excels).

Shafts were probably made from ash, although hickory was not unknown in Britain in the early eighteenth century. Thomas Kincaid, writing in 1687, stated that the shafts should be of hazel (see page 26). We are not told how many clubs the players had with them, but it seems likely that Castalio had only one iron club.

There is evidence that Scottish golfing equipment was highly regarded abroad and was exported from the seventeenth century (see p. 35). The Scots might have imported golf balls from the Low Countries from the 1490s, but in turn Dutch golfers might buy their clubs from Scotland. American Manor Court records indicate that Dutch settlers were playing golf around the present city of Albany, New York, in 1650.[4] The earliest reference to the export of golfing equipment to America is in the 'Port of Leith Collectors Book of Merchants Entrys Outwards in Midsummer Quarter, 1743', when eight dozen golf clubs and three gross (432) golf balls were shipped in the *Magdalen* to South Carolina.[5] Customs account books for Greenock in 1750 and Glasgow in 1765 show similar exports.

Further evidence of international trade in golfing equipment in the seventeenth century was uncovered in the 1970s when the wreck of the Dutch East Indiaman, the *Kennemerland*, shipwrecked off the Outer Skerries, Shetland, in 1664, was excavated. Among the pewter bottle tops, clay pipes, and lead shot, were five objects now identified as golf club heads. The heads consist of a central wooden core, around which there is a lead alloy shell. The best preserved head is marked with a group of parallel lines and crosses. These may have been purely decorative, but seem more likely to include the stamps of the club-maker and of the city in which they were made. The clubs were new when they were put on board the ship, and were probably carried for trading purposes rather than being part of the luggage of an individual. Interestingly, three of the clubs were intended for left-handed play.[6]

As might be expected, in addition to exporting golfing equipment, when Scots golfers left their own country they took their game with them. One such was Alexander Carlyle. Born in 1722, Carlyle was the son of the Minister of Prestonpans in East Lothian. After graduating from Edinburgh University he studied at Glasgow and Leyden Universities before being ordained Minister of Inveresk, Mus-

Port of Leith Collectors Book of Merchants Entrys Outwards in Mid-summer Quarter, 1743. Eight dozen golf clubs and three gross golf balls (432) were exported from Leith to South Carolina aboard the Magdalen *in 1743. (National Archives of Scotland, E5/22/1)*

selburgh, in 1748. Carlyle was friendly with many of the leading literary figures of the day and a keen supporter of the arts. His *Autobiography* gives the impression of a genial, cultured and liberal man.[7] Unfortunately, his great love of the theatre led him to fall foul of the Church establishment. Carlyle made several transcripts of *Douglas*, a play by his friend John Hume, and attended rehearsals and even a performance. For this he was censured by the Synod of Lothian and Tweeddale. Nevertheless he remained Minister of Inveresk until his death in 1805.

While in London for his sister's wedding in 1758, Carlyle regularly met his Scottish friends, including John Hume, William Robertson the historian, and the architects Robert and James Adam, for theatre visits and dinner. On one occasion the friends were invited to the house of David Garrick the actor, for dinner at his Hampton villa and a round of golf.

Unfortunately, there is no description of the actual game. After they had played, the party went on to Garrick's villa where they met with Mrs Garrick, 'a woman of uncommon good sense'. While the company waited in the garden for dinner, Carlyle showed off his golfing skills and records his prowess with a notable lack of modesty:

Sir Henry Raeburn,
*Rev. Alexander
Carlyle, 1722-
1805. Divine and
pamphleteer* [detail].
(Scottish National
Portrait Gallery)

Having Observed a Green Mound in the Garden opposite the
archway, I said to our Landlord, that While the Servants were
preparing the Collation in the Temple I would surprise him with
a stroke at the Golph, as I should Drive a Ball thro' his archway
into the Thames, once in three strokes. I had measured the
Distance with my Eye in walking about the Garden, and accordingly at the 2nd stroke made the Ball alight in the Mouth of the
Gateway, and Roll down the Green Slope into the River. This
was so Dextrous that he was quite surprised, and beg'd the Club
of me, by Which such a Feat had been perform'd.[8]

*He had told us to bring
Golph Clubs and Balls,
that we might play at that
Game on Molesly Hurst.
As we pasd thro' Kensign-
ton [sic] the Coldstream*

*Regt. were changing
Guard, and seeing our
Clubs they gave us 3 cheers
in Honour of a Diversion
Peculiar to Scotland ... we
cross'd the River to the*

*Golphing Ground w[hich]
was very Good. None of
the Company could play
but J. Home and myself
and Parson Black from
Aberdeen.*[8]

84

Living close to Musselburgh Links as Minister of Inveresk for over 50 years, it is hardly surprising Carlyle was a golfer. Interestingly, he informs us that other Scots in the party, including Robert and James Adam, did not know how to play. The implication in the *Autobiography* is that, in the mid-eighteenth century, golf in England was still considered to be a Scottish rather than an English game.

Sir John Foulis's accounts mention a 'company' of golfers playing on Leith Links in the 1680s (see chapter on 'Sir John Foulis of Ravelston', pages 47-51), and the origins of the Golf Clubs probably lie in such informal gatherings. It is difficult to be precise about the date of founding of individual Clubs due to lack of documentary evidence, but it was in the 1740s that the earliest Clubs were established and the process began of transforming what had been a largely informal game into a highly organised sport.

NOTES

1 'Emulous', i.e. in a spirit of eager rivalry.

2 Anon: *Memoirs of Duncan Forbes of Culloden* (Edinburgh, *c*.1748).

3 C. B. Clapcott, in his commentary on *The Goff* (National Library of Scotland, MS.3999), has identified 'Castalio' as Alexander Dunning, an Edinburgh bookseller, and 'Pygmalion', the loser of the match, as the author Thomas Mathison himself.

4 van Hengel, p. 66.

5 National Archives of Scotland, E5/22/1.

6 C. T. C. Dobbs and R. A. Price: 'The Kennemerland site. An Interim Report. The sixth and seventh seasons, 1952 and 1957, and the identification of five golf clubs', in *The International Journal of Nautical Archaeology*, vol. 20, no. 2 (May 1991), pp. 110-22.

7 Alexander Carlyle's *Autobiography* (National Library of Scotland, MSS.23911-16). See *The Autobiography of … Dr Alexander Carlyle, Minister of Inveresk*, edited by John Hill Burton (Edinburgh, 1860).

8 Alexander Carlyle's *Autobiography* (National Library of Scotland, MS.23915).

Prize of the Silver Golf at Edr 1787.

THE FIRST
'RULES OF GOLF'

EDINBURGH

1744

In the 1680s Sir John Foulis and his golfing companions met together on Leith Links for healthy exercise and convivial company. Although individual golfers challenged each other and made wagers, there were no formal written guidelines as to how they played. The outcome of each game was determined by the players themselves and these matches did not form part of a wider competition. This may have changed by 1743, as in his poem *The Goff*, celebrating golf on Leith Links, Thomas Mathison refers to the golfers' 'labours to obtain the bays of conquest, and the bowl to gain' (see previous chapter). Whether or not the '*Caledonian* Chiefs' of the poem were competing for a prize, we may never know. What is certain is that by the mid-eighteenth century, organised contests were associated with a number of popular sports.

Such competitions were usually sponsored by the burghs and involved their leading citizens. The competition for the Kirkcudbright Silver Gun of 1587 is the earliest known sporting contest in Scotland. In the seventeenth century, the prize of the Lanark Silver Bell was awarded for horse-racing, and archery competitions were sponsored by the towns of Musselburgh, Peebles and Selkirk. In Edinburgh, the Town Council sponsored an archery competition for a Silver Arrow from 1709. This

OPPOSITE
David Allan, *The Procession of the Silver Club*, 1787 [detail]. This drawing by David Allan depicts the ceremonial intimation through the streets 'by Tuck of Drum' of the competition for the Silver Club. (National Gallery of Scotland)

competition is particularly significant for golf history in that it was established following a request from a sporting club.

His Majesty's Company of Archers (later Royal Company of Archers) was formed in Edinburgh in 1676 as a private archery club, and is the earliest known sporting club to be formally organised with agreed rules and regulations and appointed leaders. Members competed annually for trophies, including the Edinburgh Silver Arrow from 1709 and the Silver Bowl from 1720. The Silver Arrow was shot for over Leith Links, and the competition was advertised 'by tuck of the drum' (i.e. beating the drum throughout the town). The arrow was carried formally in procession to Leith Links, and afterwards presented to the winner to keep for a year. A silver badge bearing his name, crest and motto was fixed to it.

Many of the '*Caledonian* Chiefs' of *The Goff*, such as the surgeon John Rattray, were also archers, and their experiences as archers must have influenced the formation of the first golf clubs. Rattray was born in 1709 in Perthshire, the son of Thomas Rattray, Episcopal Bishop of Dunkeld. Where he learned to shoot and play golf is not known, but he was in Edinburgh as a medical student by 1728. Rattray joined the Royal Company of Archers in 1731, winning their silver bowl for the first time in 1732. He won this three more times and was twice winner of their highest award, the Silver Arrow. Rattray was also a golfer of note and is singled out by Thomas Mathison for his 'skill'.[1]

On 7th March 1744, the year after *The Goff* was published, an 'Act of Council' of Edinburgh Town Council records that 'Several Gentlemen of Honour, Skilfull in the Ancient and Healthfull Exercise of the Golf, had from time to time applied to the Several Members of Council for a Silver Club to be annually plaid for on the Links of Leith'. The 'Act' records that, in response, the Council had asked the 'Gentlemen Golfers' to draw up 'Such Articles and Conditions, as to them Seem'd most Expedient, as proper Regulations' for a golf competition. The 'Conditions' follow. They are both detailed and specific, and were clearly drafted by men who knew the game of golf well.[2]

The competition for the Silver Club was to be open to 'Noblemen or Gentlemen, or other golfers, from any part of Great Britain or Ireland', paying 'Five Shilling Sterling' and recording their names in the eight days preceding the match 'in a Book to be provided for that purpose, which is to lye in Mrs Clephen's house in Leith'. This 'house' was the tavern run by the widow of John Clephane, a noted club-maker, and was a popular gathering place for the Leith golfers. As with the Silver Arrow, the competition was to be announced throughout the town 'by tuck of the drum', and, on the day, taken in procession to Leith Links.

There are also detailed arrangements for the order of play. Pairs of names were to be drawn out of a 'bonnet', with the first name drawn playing in the first match. In future contests this would be the privilege of the previous year's winner. Players were not to be trusted to record their own scores. Rather, a 'Clerk' was to go out with each pair to 'mark down every stroke …. And when the Match is ended, a Scrutiny of the Whole Clerk's Books or Jottings is to be made, and the player who shall appear to have won the greatest Number of Holes shall be declared the Winner of the Match.' What is not stated is how many holes or rounds of the course were to make up the match. There were then only five holes on the course at Leith and, as in *The Goff*, matches usually consisted of four circuits. Perhaps it was not thought necessary to state this.

Leith Links was then a public thoroughfare and, as such, used by a wide range of people, vehicles and animals. This must have been a source of much annoyance and hindrance for the golfers. The 'Act of Council' lays down that 'Coaches, chaises or other Wheel Machines or people on Horseback' should confine themselves to the 'High Roads' and keep off the links themselves 'when the match for the Silver Club is a-playing, or at any other times'. Clearly, this ruling was something sought after by the golfers.

The Act of Council authorises the Town's Treasurer 'to cause make

Copy of the Act of Council, 7 March 1744, of Edinburgh Town Council from the minute book of the Honourable Company of Edinburgh Golfers. (National Library of Scotland, Acc.11208/1 and The Honourable Company of Edinburgh Golfers)

a silver club not exceeding the value of fifteen pounds sterling'. In spite of this call for prudence, the Treasurer's Accounts record the actual cost as £17 4sh 3d. Following the precedent of the Silver Arrow, the Silver Club was to remain the property of the Council, but would be given to the winner to keep until the next competition; a gold or silver piece containing the winner's details was to be fixed to the Club. There was also a cash prize, with 'the crowns given in at the signing' presented to the winner.

Again, following the precedent of the Silver Arrow, 'the victor was to be called the Captain of the Golf'. This was a privileged position with responsibility for the 'Care and Inspection of the Links' and the right to 'Complain to the Lord Provost and Magistrates of any Encroachments made up them by Highroads or otherwise'. He was also to be responsible for deciding all 'Disputes touching the Golf, amongst Golfers'. While the Act did not seek to regulate how the competition should be played, what it did do is to decree that this should be the prerogative of the 'Captain of Golf' and two other players.

The first minute book of the Company of Gentleman Golfers opens with a transcription of the 'Act of Council'.[3] The first Monday in April had been fixed for the annual date of the competition and the first contest took place on 2nd April 1744. The minute book records: 'The Silver Club having been played for, Mr John Rattray Surgeon in Edinburgh, after comparing the several Clerks Jottings, is Declared to have won the same.' The entry is signed by John Rattray and witnessed by the other competitors.

Rattray, the distinguished archer and golfer, won the Silver Club for a second time in 1745. Then fate intervened and he became embroiled in the Jacobite Rising as surgeon to Prince Charles Edward Stuart. He was present at the Jacobite victory at the Battle of Prestonpans in September 1745, and followed his Prince to England and on the retreat from Derby in early 1746. He surrendered to Government supporters following the defeat at Culloden and was sent to London. After signing the Oath of Obedience he was allowed to return to Scotland. In 1751 Rattray competed for and won the Silver Club for a third and last time.

In the late 1750s his health declined, and by 1759 he described himself as a 'cripple'. John Rattray died in Edinburgh in 1771.[4]

The first competition as provided for under the 'Act of Council' was open to all comers. Accordingly, and probably also because not all the Leith golfers were in agreement as to how the game should be played, it was necessary to have a written code of conduct in place prior to the competition. Although undated, the 13 'Articles and Laws' entered, probably for ease of reference, in the back of the Company of Gentleman Golfers' minute book appear to have been drawn up in March 1744 for this purpose.[5] Incredibly, it seems that being at the back of the minute book, the 'Articles and Laws' were overlooked by historians of the game until Charles B. Clapcott 'discovered' them in 1937.[6]

The 'Articles and Laws' consist of twelve general rules for the game and one local rule. Some of the rules seem obvious today, but were clearly necessary at the time in case of disputes. That 'you must tee your ball within a club length of the hole', as in RULE 1, indicates that not everyone observed a minimum length for teeing off. RULE 2 specifically relates to teeing off, decreeing that, 'Your tee must be on the ground'. Thomas Kincaid's diary states that you should 'tie your Ball at first pretty high from the ground'; and Thomas Mathison refers to 'two pyramids' of sand made by Irus, the caddy, on which the golfers 'place two balls with careful eye'. Clearly some types of tees were unacceptable.

Following on, RULE 3 forbade putting down a new ball when playing a hole. Featherie balls easily became misshapen when hit so this would have given a considerable advantage. The exception, as outlined in RULE 8, permitted a replacement when a ball was lost, but at the expense of a distance penalty and a stroke.

RULE 4 covers debris such as 'stones, bones or any break club' on the course such as might break a club if hit. These could be removed from the putting green and within 'a club's length of the ball'. Water, the downfall of many golfers today as at Leith in 1744, is covered in RULE 5. Balls could be retrieved from water, dropped, and played again, but there was a penalty of a lost stroke.

Touching balls are covered in RULE 6: 'If your Balls be found anywhere

BELOW
'Articles & Laws in Playing at Golf', 1744, formulated by the Honourable Company of Edinburgh Golfers (National Library of Scotland, Acc.11208/2)

RULE 1
You must Tee your Ball, within a Club's length of the Hole.

RULE 2
Your Tee must be on the Ground.

RULE 3
You are not to change the Ball which you Strike off the Tee.

RULE 4
You are not to remove Stones, Bones or any Break Club, for the sake of playing your Ball, Except upon the fair Green, and that only within a Club's length of your Ball.

RULE 5
If your Ball come among Watter, or any wattery filth, you are at liberty to take out your Ball & bringing it behind the hazard and Teeing it, you may play it with any Club and allow your Adversary a Stroke for so getting out your Ball.

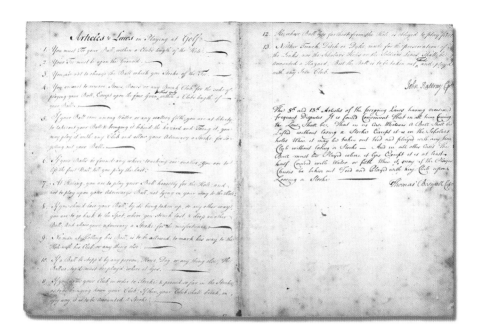

touching one another, you are to lift the first Ball till you play the last.'

RULE 7 forbids striking an opponent's ball: 'At holing, you are to play your ball honestly for the Hole, and not to play on your adversary's ball, not lying on your way to the Hole.' In both cases, that it was necessary to make the statement suggests this was common practice.

Marking the path to the hole was prohibited by RULE 9. 'No man at Holing his Ball is to be allowed to mark his way to the Hole with his Club or anything else.' This appears in most if not all eighteenth-century rules of golf and was clearly generally agreed to be important.

RULE 10 covers balls stopped 'by any person, Horse, Dog, or anything else' which were to be played where they lay.

RULE 6

If your Balls be found any where touching one another, You are to lift the first Ball, till you play the last.

RULE 7

At Holling, you are to play your Ball honestly for the Hole, and, not to play upon your Adversary's Ball, not lying in your way to the Hole.

RULE 8

If you should lose your Ball, by its being taken up, or any other way, you are to go back to the Spot, where you struck last, & drop another Ball, And allow your adversary a Stroke for the misfortune.

RULE 11 covers clubs broken in the act of striking the ball. Once the golfer brings down the club, 'If then your club shall break in any way it is to be accounted a stroke'.

RULE 12 covers the traditional practice that the player whose ball is furthest from the hole should play first.

RULE 13 is the first local rule of golf on record: 'Neither Trench, Ditch, nor Dyke made for the preservation of the Links, nor the Scholars' holes, or the Soldiers' lines, shall be accounted a Hazard, but the Ball is to be taken out, Teed and played with an Iron Club.' That no later versions of the Rules produced by the Honourable Company, including those of 1775, mention either the 'Scholars' holes' or 'Soldiers' lines', suggests these hazards were then no longer present.

Perhaps what is surprising to the modern golfer is not so much what *is* covered in the 'Articles and Laws' as what is *not*. There is nothing about the composition of either clubs or balls. The size of the hole and the green also do not feature. The principle that a ball should be played where it lies is not mentioned, perhaps because this rule was generally accepted and so, as common practice, not a matter of dispute.

The 'Articles and Laws' of 1744 were drawn up specifically for the competition for the Silver Club. Many related to what was traditional on Leith Links at the time and either endorsed or prohibited these practices. Although the rules were later subject to revisions, when the Society of St Andrews Golfers was formed in 1754, apart from the final, local 'Rule', they adopted the 'Articles and Laws' formulated by the Gentleman Golfers practically word for word. This indicates the high regard the St Andrews Golfers, later the Royal and Ancient Golf Club, had for their Edinburgh counterparts. It also demonstrates that, in spite of the difficulties of communications in mid-eighteenth century Scotland, the leading golfers in different parts of Scotland knew each other and discussed the game of golf and how it should be played.

The eighteenth-century golfing societies were very much the preserve of wealthy merchants, landowners, academics and professional men who saw golf as a means to display status, wealth and achievement, as well as a pleasant recreation: there can be no doubt that the Clubs were

RULE 9
No man at Holling his Ball, is to be allowed, to mark his way to the Hole with his club or any thing else.

RULE 10
If a Ball be stopp'd by any person, Horse, Dog, or any thing else, The Ball so stop'd must be play'd where it lyes.

RULE 11
If you draw your Club in order to Strike & proceed so far in the Stroke, as to be bringing down your Club; If then, your Club shall break, in any way, it is to be Accounted a Stroke.

RULE 12
He whose Ball lyes farthest from the Hole is obliged to play first.

RULE 13
Neither Trench, Ditch or Dyke, made for the preservation of the Links, nor the Scholar's Holes or the Soldier's Lines, shall be accounted a Hazard; But the Ball is to be taken out Teed and playd with any Iron Club.

socially exclusive. By their nature most of the personal records that survive to this day – be they letters, diaries, or account books – are papers of the wealthier members of society. Golfing equipment was expensive, and from the time of the emergence of the featherie ball in the early seventeenth century must have been beyond the pocket of the average craftsman or labourer. Golf had previously been played without expensively crafted clubs or hand-stitched balls, and there is evidence in the records of Town Councils, the Incorporations, and the Kirk Sessions, that it continued to be enjoyed by men and women from a wide range of social backgrounds. However, by the mid-eighteenth century golfing societies were proliferating in Scotland, and with their emergence the nature of the sport changed. The rules and regulations, competitions and formal social activities which developed with the Clubs took the game into another era, and were to make golf the game we know today.

NOTES

1 Colin J. L. Strachan and Jan Barker: Oxford DNB article on John Rattray (1707-1771), golfer and physician, www.oxforddnb.com

2 See Alastair J. Johnston and James F. Johnston: *The Chronicles of Golf: 1457-1857* (Cleveland [Ohio], 1993), pp. 206-18 for a detailed discussion of the 'Act of Council' of 7th March 1744.

3 Minute Book of the Company of Gentlemen Golfers, 1744-1781, National Library of Scotland, Acc.11208/1.

4 Colin J. L. Strachan and Jan Barker: Oxford DNB article on John Rattray (1707-1771), golfer and physician, op. cit.

5 'Articles and Laws in Playing at the Golf' (1744), National Library of Scotland, Acc.11208/2.

6 C. B. Clapcott, 'Honourable Company of Edinburgh Golfers (1744-1764)' (1938), National Library of Scotland, Acc.11208/66; and later published in Alastair J. Johnston (ed.): *The Clapcott Papers* (Edinburgh, 1985).

TRANSCRIPTIONS

NOTE: The transcriptions which follow provide the full text of the golf-related passages of many of the key documents featured in this book. In some cases, modern translations are also provided. A special presentation box set of facsimiles is being produced in tandem with the book by The Treasured Library, Dallas, Texas.

Act of Parliament of Scotland, 6 March 1457
National Archives of Scotland, PA5/5, f.43v

Item it is ordanyt and decretyt that Wapinschawing [displays of archery] be haldin be ye lordis and baronys spirituale and temporale four tymes in ye yeir. And [th]at ye fute bawe and ye golf be uterly cryt done and not usyt And [th]at ye bowe markes be maid at all parochkirks a pair of butts And schuting be usyt ilk Sunday .... And touchand ye futebaw and ye golf We ordane tit to be punyst be ye baronys unlaw. And if he tak it not to be tain be ye kings officars.

TRANSLATION
Item, it is ordained and the decreed that the lords and barons both spiritual and temporal should organise archery displays four times in the year. And that football and golf should be utterly condemned and stopped. And that a pair of targets should be made up at all parish churches and shooting should be practised each Sunday .... And concerning football and golf, we ordain that [those found playing these games] be punished by the local barons and, failing them, by the King's officers.

Act of Parliament of Scotland, 6 May 1471
National Archives of Scotland, PA/2/1, f.67r

It is thocht expedient [th]at ... ye futebal and golf be abusit in tym cumyng and ye buttes maid up and schot usit efter ye tenor of ye act of parlyament.

TRANSLATION
It is thought necessary that ... football and golf be abandoned in future and that targets should be made up and shooting practised according to the meaning of the Act of Parliament.

Act of Parliament of Scotland, 18 May 1491
National Archives of Scotland, PA/2/5. f.150r

Item it is Statut and ordanit ... that in na place of the realme be usit fut bawis gouff or uther sic unprofitable sportes bot for common gud and defence of the realme be hantit bowis schuting and markis therefore ordnait in ilke paraochin under ye pane of xl [forty] sh[illings] to be rasit be the schref and bailzies forsaid.

TRANSLATION
Item it is Statute and ordained ... that no part of the country should football, golf,

or other such pointless sports be practised but, for the common good and for the defence of the country, archery should be practised and targets made up in each parish under penalty of 40 shillings to be collected by the Sheriffs and Bailiffs as previously ordained.

Accounts of the Lord High Treasurer for Scotland, 22 February 1506
National Archives of Scotland, E21/7, f.192v

Item   for xii [12] golf ballis to ye king
                             iiii [4] shillings

Accounts of the Lord High Treasurer for Scotland, 22 July 1506
National Archives of Scotland, E21/7, f.141r

Item   for ii [2] golf clubbes to ye king
                             ii [2] shillings

Letters of Licence to James Melville, 1618
National Archives of Scotland,
PS 1/87, ff.169-170

f.169r

Ane L[ett]re maid makand mentioun That oure Souerane Lord understanding that thair is no small quantitie of gold and silver transported yeirlie out of his hienes kingdome of Scotland for bying of golf ballis, usit in that kingdome for Recreat[ioun] of his maj[esties] subjectis, and his hienes being earnestlie dealt w[ith] by James Melvill, in favors of Williame Bervick and his associate, who onlie makis, or can mak golf ballis within the said kingdome for the p[rese]nt, and were the inbringeris off ye said trade thair: The

said James Melvill undertaking by them and uther puir peopill (who now for lack of calling wantis maintenance),

A Letter written and finished mentions that our Sovereign Lord [King James VI and I] is aware that considerable quantities of gold and silver are taken out of His Highness's kingdom of Scotland every year to buy golf balls [which are] used in that kingdom for recreation by His Majesty's subjects. His Highness is entreated by James Melvill on behalf of William Bervick and his business partner, who are the only makers or [people who] can make golf balls in the said kingdom at present, and who are responsible for the said trade [i.e. the imports of golf balls]. The same James Melvill has made an undertaking on behalf of them and other poor people (who for want of employment are now in need of support),

f.169v

whome he shall adjoyne to the said William Bervick and his associate, to furnische the said kingdome with better golf ballis, and at ane moir easie rate then have beine sauld there these manie yeiris bypast: In consideratioun whairof, his ma[jes]tie bothe tendring the generall weill of his subjectis and increase of vertew within his said kingdome, Giving and granting unto the said James Melvill, with William Bervick and his said associate, and sik utheris as the said James Melvill shall adjoyne to them, onlie libertie to mak golf ballis within the said kingdome for the spaice of tuentie ane yeiris allanerlie, dischareging all utheris alsweill of making and selling of any golf ballis maid within the kingdome

Bot those that ar maid by the said James, his servantis, and William Bervick and his associate: Provyding allwayis, that the said ~~James his servantis~~ merchandise sall not be restrainit from importing and selling the said golfe ballis so brocht home or maid by the saidis patentis: Provyding lykwayis, that the saidis patentaris exceed not the pryce of four schillingis mo[ne]y of this realme for everie ane of the saidis golfe ballis as for the pryce thairof: And to the effect the said James and his associates may have the benefits of his ma[jes]ties grant, his hienes by these pre[se]ntis dothe expresslie prohibite and dischairge and forbid all and sindrie his ma[jes]ties subjectis, and uther persounes whatsymever, that nane of them presume, nor tak upone hand, to mak or sell anie golf ballis maid within the said kingdome, utheris then the said James Melvill and his deputies, with the said William Bervick and his associate, for the spaice foirsaid, or to utter of sell the samyne to his hienes subjectis upone whatsymever collour or pretence, under the paine of escheitting of all suche ballis so to be maid or sauld: The ane half of the benefitte aryssing thairby to come to our soverane Lordis use, and the uther half to the use of the said James Melvill and his assignayis onlie: And that the said L[ett]re be extendit in the best forme, with all clauses neidfull, With power in the samyn to the said James, by himself, his deputies, and servantis in his name to

and whom he will bring together [to work with] William Bervick and his business partner to provide the said kingdom with better golf balls and at a cheaper rate than have been sold there for many years past.

Considering this, His Majestie, thinking both of the general well-being of his subjects and of increasing the virtue of his kingdom, gives and grants to the same James Melvill, with William Bervick and his business partner, and others who James Melvill shall appoint to work with them, the only rights to make golf balls within the said kingdom for the period of twenty-one years only. [The King] also forbids all others from making and selling any golf balls made within with the kingdom except those that are made by the said James, his servants and William Bervick and his business partner. [That is] providing always that the said merchants shall not be prevented from importing and selling golf balls brought home or made under the said patent. [Also] providing likewise that the said patents do not exceed the price of four shillings money of this realm for every one of the said golf balls as the price for them. And in order that the said James and his business partners have the benefit of His Majesty's grant, His Highness hereby expressly prohibits, discharges and forbids every one of His Majesty's subjects, and all other persons whatsoever, that none of them should presume, nor take upon themselves to make or sell any golf balls made within the said kingdom, other than the said James Melvill and his deputies, with the said William Bervick and his business partner, for the period aforesaid, or to speak of or sell the same to His Highness's subjects for any reason whatsoever, under pain of confiscation of all the balls so made or sold. Half of the profit from this business is to go to our Sovereign Lord and the other half to James Melvill and those he has chosen to work with and no one else. The Letter

should be written out in the best form
and with all the necessary clauses. It
should give power to the said James, by
himself, and his deputies and servants in
his name to

f.170r

seirche, seik, and apprehend all sik golf
ballis as are maid or sauld within his
hienes said kingdome utherwayis then
according to the trew meaning of his
ma[jes]ties grant, and to eschiet the
samyn in maner above specifeit. And for
the better tryell heirof, his ma[jes]ties
ordanes the said James Melvill to have
ane particular stamp of his awin, and to
cause mark and stamp all suche ballis
maid be him and his forsaidis thairwith;
and that all ballis maid within the kingdome found to be utherwayis stamped
shall be escheated in maner foirsaid.
Given at our court of Salisbery the fifth
day of August the yeir of God sixteen
hundred and auchtenie yeiris.

TRANSLATION

search for, seek out and take possession of
all golf balls that are made or sold within
His Highness's kingdom in any way other
than according to the true meaning of His
Majesty's grant and to confiscate them as
specified above. And, to better enforce
this, His Majesty ordains that the said
James Melvill should have us own stamp,
and that all balls made by him and by
those working with and for him should
be marked and stamped with this. All
balls made within the kingdom that are
found to be stamped in otherways shall
be confiscated in the manner described
above. Given at our court of Salisbury on
the fifth day of August in the year of God
sixteen hundred and eighteen.

Act of Council and Regulations, to be observed by those, who play Yearly for, The City of Edinburgh's Silver Club

Edinburgh Town Council Minutes, Edinburgh
City Archives

p.206

7th March 1744

[Regulations for playing for the City's
Silver Club]

It being Represented in Council, That
Se[ver]all Gentlemen of Honour, Skillfull
in the anciennt and healthfull Exercise of
the Golf, Had from time to time applied
to seaverall of the members of the Council
for a silver Club to be annually playd

p.207

Playd for on the Links of Leith, at such
Time, and upon such Conditions, as the
Magistratts and Council Should think
proper: And it being Reported, That the
Gentlemen Golfers had drawn up a Scroll,
at the Desire of the Magistratts, of Such
Articles and Conditions, as to them Seemd
most Expedient, as proper Regulations to
be observed by the Gentlemen who Should
yearly offer to play for the said Silver
Club which were produced and read in
Councill the Tenor whereof Follows.

1. "As many Noblemen or Gentlemen or
   other Golfers, from any part of Great
   Brittain or Ireland as shall Book themselves Eight Days before, or upon any of
   the lawful Days of the Week Immediatly
   preceeding The Day appointed by the
   Magistrates and Council for the Annual
   Match, Shall have the Priviledge of playing for the said Club, Each Signer paying
   Five Shilling Sterling at Signing, in a Book
   to be provided for that purpose, which is
   to ly in Mrs Clephen's House in Leith, or

Such other House as afterwards the Subscribers shall appoint from year to year; and the Regulations approved of by The Magistrates and Council shall be recorded at the beginning of said Book.

2. "On the Morning before playing small Bits of paper marked with the Figures 1, 2, 3, etc., According to the number of Players shall be put into a Bonnet, and drawn by the Signers, and every Couple shall be matched according to the Figures By them drawn, Beginning with Number 1, 2, and so on; but if there shall be a great Number of Subscribers they shall be matchd in Threes; And after the Parties are thus Matched, in case there be an odd Number, the Gentleman who draws it shall play along with the last Set.

3. "After the Figures are drawn, the Set or Match beginning with No. 1, etc., shall go out first, with a Clerk to mark down every Stroke each of them shall

p.208
Shall take to Every Hole; then, by the Time They are at the Sawmill Hole, the Second Set, beginning with No. 3, or 4 According as the Match shall be made, shall strike off; and so all the rest in the same order, Each set haveing a Clerk: And when the Match is Ended, a scrutiny of the whole Clerks Books or Jotings is to be made, And the Player who shall appear to have won the greatest Number of Holes shall be Declared to be the Winner of the Match; And if there shall be Two, Three, or more, that are Equal, then these Two or Three, etc. must play a Round themselves, in the Order of their Figures, before they Go off the Ground, to Determine the Match.

4. "The Crowns Given in are solely to be at the Disposal of the Victor.

5. "Every Victor is to append a Gold or Silver peice, as he pleases, to the Club, for the Year he Wins.

6. "That Every Victor shall, at the receiving the Club, give sufficient Caution to the Magistrates and Council of Edinburgh for Fifty pounds Sterl[ing], for delivering back the Club to their Hands One Month before it is to be playd for again.

7. "That the Club is declared to be allways the Property of the Good Town.

8. That if any Dispute shall happen betwixt any of the parties, the same shall be determined by the other Subscribers not Concern'd in the Debate.

9. That the Victor shall be called **Captain of The Golf**, and all Disputes touching the Golf amongst Golfers shall be Determined by the Captain, and any Two or Three of the Subscribers he shall call to his assistance And that The Captain shall be intituled next year to the first ticket without drawing.

10. That no Coaches Chaises or other wheel ma-
p.209
machins, or people on horseback, are to be allowed to goe through the Links, but by the high Roads, when the Match for the Silver Club is a playing, or at any other time, And that the said Captain shall from year to year, have the Care and Inspection of the Links, and shall be at Liberty to Complain To the Lord Provost and Magistrates of any Encroachments made upon them by Highroads or otherwise.

99

11. The Subscribers shall have power, if the Day appointed for the Match shall be improper for playing it, to adjourn to another Day, Upon Which, if it is fit for playing, the Match shall proceed.

Lastly, It is Declared, That, Upon no pretence whatsoever, The City of Edinburgh shall be put to any Sort of Expense upon account of playing for the said Club annually, except to Intimate by Tuck of Drum, through the City the day upon which It shall be Annually playd for, such Time before the Match as the Magistrates and Council shall think proper, And to send the Silver Club to Leith upon the morning appointed for the Match.

Which Regulations having been Considered By the Magistrates & Council, They with the Extraordinary Deacons approved thereof with & under this express Condition, that nothing Contain in the above Regulations Shall in any Sort Prejudge the Magistracy & Council to Dispose in feu or otherwise of all or any part of the Links of Leith as they shall think proper. And they hereby Authorize The Treasurer to Cause make a Silver Club not Exceeding the value of fifteen pounds Sterling, to be playd for annually upon the above Conditions With Power to the Captain of the Golf, and any two of the subscribers to make such orders of the Regulating and manner of playing from time to time, as they shall think proper.

p.210

proper. And Do hereby appoint the first Monday of Aprile yearly as the Day for playing the Annual Match for the Silver Club.

John Coutts Provost

Port of Leith Collectors Book of Merchants Entrys Outwards in Midsummer Quarter 1743
National Archives of Scotland, E504/22/1

In the Magdalen William Carse Ma[ste]r for South Carolina

No 10 12 May 1743
In the Magdalen predict

David Deas

5 bundles qh [containing] 20 [piec]es, containing 757 Yards, being 605 1/2 Elks British made Sailcloth, & fit to be made into Sails p[er] assed[ation]. 2 boxes qh [containing] 8 dozen Golf Clubs, 3 Groce Golf balls, & 6 Shirts, also 6 Casks qh [containing] 18 bushells Scots Salt, which came here from Anstr[uther] p[e]r permit of the 11th May instant, free.

Thomas Kincaid's diary, 1687-1688
National Library of Scotland, Adv.MS.32.7.7

f.5v

The way of playing at the Golve. Jan 20

after dinner I went out to the Golve with Hen[ry] Legatt. I found that the only way of playing at the Golve is

1. to stand as you do at fenceing with the small sword, bending your legs a little and holding the muscles of your legs and back and armes exceeding bent or fixt or stiffe, and not at all slackning them in the time you are bringing down the Stroak (which you readily doe.)

2. the ball most be straight before your breast, a little towards the left foot.

3. your left foot most stand but a little before the right, or rather it most be even with it, and at a convenient distance from it,

4. ye most lean most to the right foot,
5. but all the turning about of your body most be only upon your legs holding them as stiff as ye can.
6. then ye most incline your body a little forward from the small of the back and upwards; for seeing all the strength of the stroake is from the swing of the body in turning about, then certainly the further forward you incline your body or shoulders they most have the greater swing, and consequently give the greater stroak, but you most not incline so fare forward as that it make you stand the more unstedfastly and waver a little in bringing down the stroak.
7. you most keep your body in

f.6r

Jan 20 the way of playing at the golve.

this posture all the time both in bringing back the club and forward, that is, you most nither raise your body straighter in bringing back the club nor incline it further in bringing down the club, but ye most bring back the club by turning yourself about to the right hand, and that as it were upon a center, without moveing your body out of the place of it, but only in chainging the position of it in thrawing it about or turning it about upon that center, so then ye most cast the weight of your body off the on[e] leg on the other in the time you are bringing about the club: neither most you in the least turn down your left shoulder and up your right in bringing back the club, thinking therby to give the club a larger swinge, and so incresse its force or to raise the ball: for it is a verie unsettled motion that throw of the body whereby you turn down the left shoulder and up the right, so that

therby you will verie often misse the ball, and almost never hitt it exactly.
8. your armes most move but verie little, all the motion most be performed with the turning of your body about. The armes serve only to guid the club and to second and carie on that motion imprest upon it by turning of your body therefore ye most never begin to bring about the club with the motion of the armes first, but their motion most be only towards the end of the stroak.

f.6v

the way of playing at the golve: Jan 20

9. all the motion of the armes most be at the shoulder and all the motion of the legs most be at the upmost joint at the loyns.
10. you most make no halt or rest, which is a slackning of the muscles of the back, between the bringing back of the club and the bringing it forward, but bring it about with that swiftness that the naturall swing of the club requires holding it pretty fast in your hands. In every motion the muscles that concur to the performing at golve keep bent and stayd which in all motions of your armes you will be helped to do by contracting your fingers, and so if there be anything in your hand you most grip verie fast.
11. you most aim directly to hit the ball it selfe, and not aim to scum the ground or strick close to the ground; thinking that then you are sure to hitt it, for this is but ane indirect way of hitting the ball neither is it sure when the balls lies inconveniently; neither 3dly is it exact, for you will butt seldome hitt the ball exactly and cleanly this way; and 4ly it is more difficult then the other way, whereas the other way is more easie. 2, sure, 3, better for

hitting the ball exactly. The way to learn this is to tie your ball at first pretty high from the ground.

12. the shaft of your club most be of hazel. your club most be almost straight that is the head most make a verie obtuse angle with the shaft, and it most bend as much at the handle as it doth at the wooping, being verie supple and both long and Great.

13. Your ball most be of a middle size nither to[o] big nor too little, and then the heavier it is in respect of its bigness it is still the better. It most be of thick and hard leather not with pores or grains or that will lett a

f.7r

whether it be better that the in equality of gamsters be remedied in the game or in the stakes.

pin easily passe through it especially at the soft end. I came in with Hen[ry] And John Pringle we mett with John Corss and went in to a change house called Willsons we stayed till 11 of the clock Hen[ry] payd 49 shill[ings] I payd 13 shill[ings] John Corss payd 7 shill[ings].

21 Freed. I rose at 7. I thought upon this way of playing at Golve. I ex. till 9. I wrott this till 8 of the clock at night. I thought upon the question whither it is better in giveing advantadge in gameing to make the game equall, and the stakes unequall, or to make the stakes equall and give some advantadge in the game, as at the glove whither it is better to give a man two holes of three; laying equall stakes, or to lay three stakes to his on[e] and play equall for so much every hole. For answer we most distinguish between

the giving a man so great advantadge as to putt him within on[e] hazard of the game, and the putting him only within two or three hazards of the game. For the worst of gamesters may readily winne on[e] hazard but the[y] will hardly win two or three in on[e] game. For solution then of the question we say, that if the game depend upon on[e] hazard it is all on whither ye make the inequality in the stakes or in the game. But if the game consist of more hazards then on[e], it is by farre securer for the giver of the advantadge to make the inequality rather in the stakes then in the game. For when the game is equall and depends on many hazards it is almost all

f.7v

the necessity and way of hitting the ball exactly   Jan 21

it is almost alltogether improbable that a bad player will gain it on[ce] in 20 times, whereas if he gett the advantadge in the game, he may be fair to win it every time, at least he will readily win it at some time. Therefore with these that are worst gamesters than yourselfe make always the game depend upon mo[r]e hazards then on[e], and the mo[r]e the better, but with these that are better gamesters make always the game to depend upon on[e] hazard.

I found that the first point to be studied in playeing at the golve is to hitt the ball exactly; for if you hitt the ball exactly though the club have butt little strength yett the ball will fly verie farre. The way to attain this perfection is to play with little strenth at first but yet acuratly observeing all the rules of poustaur [posture] and motion before sett down,

and then when ye have acquired ane
habit of hitting the ball exactly ye most
learn to increase your strenth or force in
the stroak by degrees, staying still so long
upon every degree till you have acquired
ane habit of it; neither will the knowl-
edge of these degrees be altogither uselese
afterward, for they will serve for halfe
chops, and quarter chops and for holling
the ball. But then in going through all
these degrees of strenth you most be verie
attentive and carefull not to alter that
postaur of your body of [or] way of moveing and bringing about the club, which
ye observed when ye playd with little
strenth for the

f.8r

that the greatest and strongest motion
most begin first.

for the only reason why men readily miss
the ball when they strick with more strenth
then ordinare is because their incressing
their strenth in the stroak makes them
alter their ordinare position of their body
and ordinare way of bringing about the
club, as also it makes them stand much
more unsetledly and waver in bringing
about the club, and so they readily miss
the ball. I found that I n all motion the
greatest and the strongest motion most
begin first ...

f.11r

24 [Jan] Moond[ay] I rose at 4 and ex.
till 5 I wrott this and thought on severall
things till 8 as of the way of standing at
the Golve, that your feet most be both of
ane equall distance from the ball at least
the ball most ly [lie] upon a line that is
perpendicular to that line that passeth between the on[e] foot and the other. These

places will be found by drawing a circle
round about the ball which most be the
center and placeing your feet on that circle,
that your feet most not stand parallel to
the way you would have the ball to fly,
but upon a line declineing towards the
left hand as it were 10 or 15 degrees ...

f.11v

Jan 25, 26 some particulars of the
motion of playing at the glove

25. Tuesd[ay] I rose at 5 I wrote the
analysis of some psalms till 7 I wrott all
the remarks out of Glasar's Compleat
Chymist till 11. I glewed the club head
and sat with   Mr Crawford I boyld the
unguentum album with vinagar I read
some of Berbett de fractures et luxation-
ibus. After dinner I took out the plains
and made a little skelpe to putt on the
club. I took of[f] the piece that was joynd
to the old shaft . I glewed too that skelpe
till 3. I read Berbett de ambustione, and
some other places of him till 4. James
Duncan came in and sat till 6 ...

26. Wed[nesday] I rose at 7 ...

I thought on the playing at the Golve.

1. I found that ye most rest most upon the
right legg for the most part, but yet not
too much as to be exactly perpendicular
upon it, which ye will know by the
ballanceing of your body.

2. I found that the club most always move in
a circle making ane angle of 45 degrees
with the horizon.

3. that the whole turning of your body about
most be by thrawing the joints of your
right legg and then when .... [MS torn]
you most throw the

small of your back so that the left
shoulder will turn a little down wards,
because the body is inclines a little
forward, but ye most beware of raising
the on[e] shoulder higher than the other
as to their position in the body, for that
motion is not convenient for this action.

4. I found that in bringing down the club ye
most turn your body as farr about towards
the left following the swinge of the club
as it had been turned before towards the
right hand.

5. I found that seeing the swinge of your
body by the turning it upon your legg is
the largest and strongest motion, therefor
it most begin first, and the turning at the
small of the back most only second it,
and then most follow the motion at the
shoulders. The other motions most be
but verie little and imperceptible, neither
most these motions at the small of the
back and shoulders, being till the club have
hitt the ball or at least be verie near it. I
thought on these and wrott them till 5.
James Craige came in and sat till 7 …

27 Jan Thurs[day] I rose at 7 I thought
on severall things … I joynd a piece to
the shaft of the club till 4 …

4. … I found that the making a club waver
in bringing it back did make you add a
great deal more force to it in bringing it
foreward then otherways you can get
added to it. The way to make the club
waver in bringing it up is by drawing in
your armes and hands close to your breast,
and the reason that this postaur adds
more strenth to the stroake is because the
further out that you streatch your armes
they are still the weaker, and the closers
to your breast they are the stronger …

….

8. Tuesd[ay] I thought upon the way of
ordering pathology and of distinguishing
it into its proper parts and at good method
… Hen[ry] Legatt came in an desired me
out to the golve. I putt on my cloths and
went to him. He bought a club in Captain
Fosters we went down to Leath in a Coach
which was 10 shill[ings] We played till 5.
I bought three balls 14 shill. We went in
to Captain browns were we satt till 6

waiting on the coach but could not get it,
we came up to John watts where we gott
some collips I spent 14 shill[ings] and
was exceeding seek.

9. Wed[nesday] I rose at 7 I thought upon
the method of pathologie and on playing
at the golve I found that in all motions of
your armes ye most contract your fingers
verie strait and grip fast any thing that is
in them for that doth command the
motion exactly, and keeps all the muscles
of the arme verie bent. I digested the rules
of playing at the golve into verse thus.

Gripe fast stand with your left leg first not farre
Incline your back and shoulders but beware
You raise them not when back the club you
    bring
make all the motion with your bodies swinge
And shoulders, holding still the muscles bent
play slowly first till you the way have learnt
At such lenth hold the club as fitts your strenth
The lighter head requires the longer lenth.
That circle wherein moves your club and hands
At forty five degrees from th[e] horizon stands.
What at on[e] stroak to effectuat you despair
Seek only 'gainst the nist it to prepare.

Letter of Alexander Monro to John Mackenzie of Delvine, 27 April 1691

National Library of Scotland,
MS.1393, ff.177-178

f.177
Sir

...

Receive from the bearer our post ane Sett of Golfe-clubs consisting of three, viz. an play club, ane Scraper, and ane tine fac'd club. I might have made the set to consist of more: but I know not your play and if you stand in need of more I think you should call for them from me. Tho I know you may be served thear yet I presumed that such a present from this place the metropolis of Golfing may not be unsuitable for these fields especially when it's come from a friend. Upon the same consideration I have also sent you ane Dozen of Golfe balls, which receive with the clubs. I am told they are good, but that will prove according to your play and the fields. If the size do not suite, were you so free with me I would mend it with the next. I am glad to have any occasion to kisse your hands at a distance. And to subscribe myselfe still
St Andrews 27 April 1691

Sir
Youre faithfull and most humble servant
Al[exander] Monro

f.178
[Postscript to letter]

The bearer may have other Clubs and balls from this place but yours cannot be mistaken if you receive them marked viz The Clubs with the Lres [letters] G.M. as the tradesmans proper signe for himselfe and JMK for your markes stamped upon ilke ane of the Clubs And ilke ane of the balls are marked W.B. which are not ordinarily counterfeited.

David Wedderburn, Vocabula, Edinburgh, 1711

National Library of Scotland

BACULUS

Baculus, pila clavaria, a Golf Ball; Fovea, a Goat [bunker]; Percute pilam baculo: Nimis curtasti hunc missum, This is too short a stroak; Pila tua devia est: Procul excussisti pilam, This is a good stroak. Statumina pilam arena, Teaze [tee up] your Ball on the sand; Statumen, The Teaze; Frustra es, That is a miss, vel irritus hic conatus est. Percute pilam, sensim, Give the Ball but a little chap. Apposite, That is very well. Immissa est pila in Foveam, The Ball is goated. Quomodo eum hinc elidam. Cedo baculum ferreum. Let see the Buncard Club. Iam iterum frustra es, That is the second miss. Tertio, quarto, etc. Bene tibi cessit hic ictus, That is well sticken. Male tibi cessit hic ictus. Huc recta pilam dirige: Dirige recta versus foramen, Strike directly upon the hole. Percute pilam sursam versus, Strike up the hill: Percute deorsum versus, Strike down the hill: Ah praeterlapsa est foramen: Factum quod volui, I would not wish a better stroak; Immissa est in paludem, It is in the Myre: Recta evolavit, It hath flown directly on. Baculi caput, The head of the Club. Baculi caulis, The Club shaft. Baculi manubrium, the handle where the wippen [grip] is, Baculi filum, The wippen.

Articles & Laws in Playing at Golf, 1744
Honourable Company of Edinburgh Golfers,
National Library of Scotland, Acc.11208/2

1. You must Tee your Ball, within a Club's length of the Hole.
2. Your Tee must be on the Ground.
3. You are not to change the Ball which you Strike off the Tee.
4. You are not to remove Stones, Bones or any Break Club, for the sake of playing your Ball, Except upon the fair Green, and that only within a Club's length of your Ball.
5. If your Ball come among Watter, or any wattery filth, you are at liberty to take out your Ball & bringing it behind the hazard and Teeing it, you may play it with any Club and allow your Adversary a Stroke for so getting out your Ball.
6. If your Balls be found any where touching one another, You are to lift the first Ball, till you play the last.
7. At Holling, you are to play your Ball honestly for the Hole, and, not to play upon your Adversary's Ball, not lying in your way to the Hole.
8. If you should lose your Ball, by its being taken up, or any other way, you are to go back to the Spot, where you struck last, & drop another Ball, And allow your adversary a Stroke for the misfortune.
9. No man at Holling his Ball, is to be allowed, to mark his way to the Hole with his club or any thing else.
10. If a Ball be stopp'd by any person, Horse, Dog, or any thing else, The Ball so stop'd must be play'd where it lyes.
11. If you draw your Club in order to Strike & proceed so far in the Stroke, as to be bringing down your Club; If then, your Club shall break, in any way, it is to be Accounted a Stroke.
12. He whose Ball lyes farthest from the Hole is obliged to play first.
13. Neither Trench, Ditch or Dyke, made for the preservation of the Links, nor the Scholar's Holes or the Soldier's Lines, shall be accounted a Hazard; But the Ball is to be taken out Teed and playd with any Iron Club.

John Rattray, Cap[tai]n

The 5th and 13th Articles of the forgoing Laws having occasioned frequent Disputes It is found Convenient That in all time Coming the Law shall be, That in no case Whatever a Ball shall be Lifted without losing a Stroke Except it is in the Scholars holes When it may be taken out teed and played with any Iron Club without losing a Stroke – And in all other Cases The Ball must be Played where it lyes Except it is at least half Covered with Water or filth When it may if the Player Chuses be taken out Teed and Played with any Club upon Loosing a Stroke.

Thomas Boswall Cap[tai]n